Roots of
Financial Freedom

Roots of Financial Freedom

A Timeless Financial Planning Guide

Snjkv

PARTRIDGE

Copyright © 2019 by Snjkv.

ISBN: Hardcover   978-1-5437-0502-7
        Softcover   978-1-5437-0501-0
        eBook   978-1-5437-0500-3

All rights reserved. No part of this book may be used or reproduced by any means, graphic, electronic, or mechanical, including photocopying, recording, taping or by any information storage retrieval system without the written permission of the author except in the case of brief quotations embodied in critical articles and reviews.

Because of the dynamic nature of the Internet, any web addresses or links contained in this book may have changed since publication and may no longer be valid. The views expressed in this work are solely those of the author and do not necessarily reflect the views of the publisher, and the publisher hereby disclaims any responsibility for them.

Print information available on the last page.

To order additional copies of this book, contact
Partridge India
000 800 10062 62
orders.india@partridgepublishing.com

www.partridgepublishing.com/india

Preface

Financial planning is a beautiful and revolutionary art of the modern age, but it requires relevant knowledge, constant learning, common sense, and remarkable passion to get varieties of ideas to experiment and implement so that the plan for a financially-independent future gets closer and closer to perfection. It is not either for the affluent alone or the destitute or everyone between. Irrespective of one's personal financial position, the study of financial planning has a solution to offer, for every situation. But solutions for such challenging situations depend on the critical bent of mind of a trained and experienced professional. Throughout the book, I keep repeating what one should remember well or how one should act under certain circumstances. While I intend to impart fundamental financial education and present the right perspective to the educated and optimistic reader, I am also keen to persuade such readers that are stubborn and reluctant to accept what is considered valuable for the upliftment of their personal finances, lifestyles and consequently the society.

My object is not to turn the reader into an expert on personal finance. I only intend to give direction to beginners – individuals and professionals alike, as to how selflessly and prudently one must think and act to ensure a carefree financial future. One must understand that the brilliance of an entire lot of remarkable financial planners cannot be put into a single book. Some point or angle that may not have been mentioned in a specific section or the book does not imply that the writer is ignorant of it or overlooked it. Every scenario and alternative cannot be mentioned, explained, and addressed. Doing so will make this a comprehensive textbook in multiple volumes for a student of personal finance or an encyclopaedia but not a self-help book for the average person to understand the crux of financial planning. I also want the reader to note that I have not used too many designer graphs, images, or tables in most of the book, only to force him or her to not take the shortcut route, refer a single piece of information and ignore the relevant references surrounding it.

On finishing reading the book considerately, one will know whether one should employ the services of a professional or plan the finances oneself and what difference can a financial planner make. One will know the level of one's knowledge and whether such knowledge is enough to prepare a comprehensive plan. Remember that even if one plans the finances independently, seeking second opinion from a financial planner as one does in the case of critical health care, is recommended. It is human tendency to sometimes overvalue one's own basic knowledge of a subject and regard the proficiency of an expert as common knowledge. It is like knowing to buy aspirin from a pharmacist and believing you know a lot about the medical science surrounding headaches and migraines. Even if one has the plan prepared by a professional already, taking second opinion from another for a reasonable fee does only good but no harm. If one is sincere and keen to achieve their financial needs, given enough time, no financial need is difficult to achieve. One must merely have perseverance to stick to the plan.

Economic factors, government policies, financial products, tax laws and people's sentiments etc. may change over time but the fundamentals of personal finance and the fundamental way a financial planner should think shall never change. The crux of financial planning principle is timeless.

Contents

Preface v
Chapter Summary xi

Spirit of Financial Planning 1
   Understanding the central idea 7
      Life's Needs and Goals 10
      Commanders of Planning 16
   Foundations of the Profession 24
      Board and Network 25
      Rules of the Profession 34
Safeguarding the benefits 40
   Subject matter of solicitation 41
      Understanding Insurance 44
      General Principles 47
   Managing financial risks 54
      Critical Insurances 55
Realising needs and wants 75
   Prerequisites of investing 77
      Investment Risks 87
      Asset Classification 97
   Realising financial goals 116
      Goal Planning 117
      Notable Products 121
Sedentary Second Innings 150
   The gay retiree's inner peace 153

- Elixir of Retirement 153
- Delayed Expenditure.. 166
- Leaving a legacy behind...172
  - Love, Money, and Wisdom 173
  - Laws of succession...175
- Taxing Social Responsibilities 180
  - Obligated social responsibility 183
    - Understanding the rules..................................... 184
    - Concerning individuals....................................... 189
  - Making the best out of benefits 194
    - Deduction and Exemption 196
    - Miscellaneous Taxes..210
- Progressive Execution Guide 218
  - Learning to plan independently............................... 220
    - Meaningful Jargon... 220
    - Simple Illustration... 229
  - Keeping in shape on the track................................. 238
    - Periodic Review 239
    - Avoiding Mistakes 242
- Wrap-up... 256

Chapter Summary

Chapter 1: 'Spirit of Financial Planning' introduces to the reader, what the term truly means in the view of the writer, how various life's goals must be planned and the factors that make financial planning inevitable. It also talks about the profession, its entry into India, regulations laid down to supervise the practice and the responsibilities of a professional financial planner towards the individuals or clients seeking suitable advice for achieving their needs and goals.

Chapter 2: 'Safeguarding the Benefits' talks about various critical needs that most humans encounter, which if not suitably planned for, prove devastating on the financial and personal lives of the depending family. It also talks about the principles and diverse types of insurances one can buy for mitigating financial risks and protecting one's family's financial needs in the absence of the bread-earner or simply, contingencies.

Chapter 3: 'Realising Needs and Wants' takes references of different financial needs and goals merely mentioned in chapter one and discusses how calculatedly one should plan for them so that there will be no shortcomings when the goals are due to. It also explains how investment risk can be mitigated by adopting investment strategies including apportionment of investments and other financial products to one's goals, coordinated with their time horizon.

Chapter 4: 'Sedentary Second Innings' is a direct reference to a happy, peaceful and healthy retired life. While pension is crucial in the later years, certain major expenses causally related to old age and some needs and goals that fall due after the age of retirement pose a threat to heard earned retirement corpus if they are not identified well in advance and planned for separately. The chapter also throws some light on bequeathing estate to the loved ones after one's lifetime.

Chapter 5: 'Taxing Social Responsibilities' contains references to income tax chargeable under various sections of the Income Tax Act, 1961. The sections and provisions mentioned in the chapter are related to individuals only and not even the HUF or the Hindu Undivided Family. It also mentions various important tax deductions allowed from the total income and exemptions allowed under different heads of incomes mentioned in the Act for individuals.

Chapter 6: 'Progressive Execution Guide' is a reference guide for individuals to further improve their knowledge of personal finance and for students or enthusiastic professionals. It throws light on specific financial terms and elaborates the method of preparing a financial plan in a practical manner. A plan once prepared must not be considered final and forever. It must be reviewed periodically along with financial products if any purchased, to keep the plan and finances goal-oriented.

Spirit of Financial Planning

Since the beginning of time, mankind has been striving not merely for survival but for a better life – a life that is less worrisome (human mind has/can never be completely free from worry of some sort) and provisioning in abundance so that one need not fear what the unpredictable future holds. Of course, there are always some that crave riches and luxuries, but the majority are content with necessities. This majority worried about making both ends meet. Some needed a shelter that they could call home; some needed a family and companionship while the rest, a minority, having all other basic needs provided for abundantly, craved respect, honour, fame and pleasures. Over time, the magnitude and diversity of consequences of the disparities in lifestyles among people increased, complicating what was supposed to be a simple and happy life that primarily focused on basic needs. Today, human kind has been too deep into this chaotic fretwork that is devoid of laudable age-old traditions that even the emergence of countless god-men, spiritual leaders and motivational speakers is inadequate to bring back the lost peace and content to the mind.

Through the course of its history since the separation from its extinct ancestors what the scientists call *Homo erectus*, mankind has not advanced so fast as it did in the past two hundred years and more so in the last 20 years. Just as we do not anymore strike magnesium rocks to make fire, certain aspects of the present day living require modern and contemporary thinking and approaches to life while preserving critical cultural values, sometimes though redundant but not obsolete as they may seem. This is more relevant to the subject of personal finance as life today revolves not mostly but invariably around the magical word – *Money*.

The days of believing in the *Karma* of past lives and the consequential birth into riches or scarcity and health or sickness are fast thinning away. However, when they are understood as consequences of one's own actions, the ideas of fate and Karma appeal more to this generation and are universally accepted just as how scientists cannot explain the causes of gravity and life though they can study and explain their significance and effects. Hence, it is only rational that we make adequate provisions to counter and survive the repercussions of our uncalculated actions for, life is not a bed of roses as we all agree.

The rich and poor may be born so, but the middle-class is always made - upper or lower does not matter. We cannot say much about the generations before it, but the yester-generation certainly struggled a great deal to improve the lifestyles of its families. Some were successful while others were not. With the passage of time, the needs and priorities hanged. One may be too proud or unwilling to agree, but the failure in every case came from poor planning of finances or no planning at all. Not that they were ignorant of the needs of life or cared less for their future or of their children, but they then simply lacked the present day's modern approach to planning one's future.

The poor that were not so born were made from this band of men who did not foresee the impact of their financial decisions should they go awry. The reason could be ignorance or any but seldom luck. They bought a piece of land on the outskirts of a city or bought shares of some agrarian or other lucrative business expecting it to make them rich in no time or bought an inadequate insurance or pension plan and eventually did not make arrangements for contingencies. Others simply spent their money on luxuries at the cost of their future or gambled away while some gave away to the church or the 'have-not'. In the end, they all burnt their hands, owed money everywhere and sold everything they had until they had nothing more to lose but a mirage of a financially independent future. These men were only lucky if their offspring worked hard and made their way up to regain the family's former glory, at times at someone else's grace or friendly hand. Nevertheless, the financial mistakes of the yester-generation are pardonable as opposed to those of the present.

With the advent of the mobile phone and the internet, in this golden era of technology, even those living in far-flung areas have access to loads of information and knowledge, which should make informed-decision-making not difficult. Still, the bulk of the middle-class and the affluent alike, without the exception of educated, are uninformed about the techniques and the need for managing personal finances to achieve a smoother financial future. Even today, many understand personal finance or financial planning merely as investments or insurance or saving taxes. With all the privileges of the modern age at their disposal, the mistakes of the present generation as regards personal finances are inexcusable, while we must blame equally, the advisors, organisations and the government for such shortcomings.

Have you ever wondered why one could not pursue higher studies or if they did, why one had to apply for education loan to the bank? Have you ever given a dabble to the thought that one could have married off his/her daughter without having to mortgage a property or disposing of an asset at a loss had they planned for the need early? Do you know that one would not have had to depend on one's progeny for survival and medical expenses in their later years whether the latter was sympathetic or not to the plights of their aged parents? Through careful planning, one can make suitable provisions to meet one's financial goals and address the uncertainties of life without any (or less) difficulty or the feeling of burden when such goals are due for fulfilment.

Financial planning addresses every aspect in the life of an individual where money is involved and provides solutions to achieve various financial needs and goals. If one has a financial problem or foresees (or not) a need for money in the future, financial planning has a solution for it, if the means to achieve the needs and goals exist, if need be, with some additional effort on the part of the willing individual or the family.

But, do not get excited yet. The fruits of financial planning are not seen instantly except when urgent solutions are indispensable, but they are not related to planning. It takes awfully long years of patience and discipline for financial planning to work for us but in the end, they will transform our lives and that of the generations to come. They will change our understanding, opinion, and treatment of money. Rome was not built in a day nor did the English conquer the World in a day. Let us take an interesting example to simplify what we meant. In a typical Indian movie, it is common for a politician to file nomination for contesting in elections in the last hour on the last day. And naturally, if the politician was the protagonist, the villain caused trouble and if the politician was the villain, the hero-party hindered the former's plans. The question is, why not file the nomination in the first hour on the first day when the announcement for nomination was made? But no! They do it only in the last hour on the last day and naturally lose the fight. Alas, it is but too late. They will have to wait until the next election now.

One of the foremost challenges for an Indian parent is to get the daughter married off at the right age to an agreeable young man. In a country like India, with population over quarter-and-a-billion, even in this age of space travel and ideas of warping through space and blackholes, age-old customs still linger widely in all communities. A girl may have a very fair complexion (the outlook is only beginning to change), great looks and education, and a dexterous hand at domestic chores but all that is overlooked if her father cannot afford a handsome dowry to please his prospective son-in-law. Not worrying about the social evil now, let us recollect how many families we have seen where the parent started setting aside an asset for the wedding of the child that is due twenty-five years thence, (from the day the child was born) in spite of being aware that one day this obligation will have to be fulfilled? Would not it be easier to meet the goal if the parents planned for it as many years in advance?

One may say that it is not as simple as we put it. Granted! But one must at least take the right steps to make a difference for their future. Whatever challenges one face on their way to accomplishing a goal, financial planning addresses them and helps overcome the hurdles. True, it cannot help in finding the right groom (it does not do matchmaking) or lend money when you need some, but it surely takes the financial burden off your mind gradually, if you are willing to listen to it and follow its guidelines. Just as we do not anymore relish the old trend in movies where the police appear in the climax simply to arrest the villain after the hero undergoes all the hardships and has near-death experience, we do not also want anymore to stick to the stereotypes and later break our heads about meeting the goals effortlessly, just when they are about to knock on our front door.

What we have discussed so far are simple cases, but real life is a lot crueller. Imagine you are going for camping or travelling by train or air. What do you do? Plan the itinerary or check the vehicle and gas; make a list of items for baggage, grab some medicines for an emergency, pack some food etc., right? In financial planning, you make a similar plan; not for some outdoor sport or train travel but the journey of life that is predictable and unpredictable, ever challenging, and impossible yet wonderful if you know how to tread the path carefully. Except for a trifling percentage, people are not aware that they can be free from financial difficulties if only they seek shelter under the tree, that professionals termed as 'Financial Planning'. Let us dive into the magnificent world of planning for financial independence!

Understanding the central idea

If the reader is a novice or a nonprofessional and desires to appropriately plan his personal finances himself or educate himself sufficiently to ask a professional, right questions and confide in his impartial advice, this being a self-help book, the previous introduction requires further explanation with narratives. I prefer to define or explain Financial Planning thus –

"Financial Planning means evaluation of personal financial position of an individual or a family, identifying financial needs and choosing financial goals, and apportioning current and future assets, cash flows and time in the most rational manner to make the apportioned resources work best, and help seamlessly realize the prioritised needs and goals when they are due."

I also mentioned the word Personal Finance earlier. So, what is it and how is it different from financial planning? Are they synonymous, if so, why use two words as if to confuse the reader? Let us understand the two simple terms – personal finance and financial planning. By personal finance, we mean collection of all present and future fixed, financial, and intangible assets and liabilities, present and future cash flows and all other benefits in cash or kind one receives from employers, governments policies, inheritances, gifts etc. Studying these (individual) personal finances and strategically allocating them to various financial needs and goals constitutes financial planning. *A carefully crafted, implemented, and periodically reviewed financial plan ensures that at no point of time in the life of an individual, he/she faces any financial difficulty for,*

absolutely every need is foreseen and adequately planned for, well in advance. This definition is a disclaimer in itself, and if understood well, needs no elaboration.

The most important thing to note here is that financial planning is all about money i.e. wherever, in whichever aspect of life money is involved directly or otherwise, it becomes a subject matter of financial planning, but be careful not to mistake it to investing. Yes, investing is a significant part of the process but there is lot more to the idea than merely buying financial products that seem lucrative. Sometimes, certain aspects of life might not involve money or buying financial products at all but involve the individual's actions that will influence the finances and cash flows. Let me cite some examples here for either scenario.

Suppose you foresee a need for Rs. 5 Lakhs ten years hence. You do not have any asset to allocate now and sell it when the need is due. The only provision you can make for this need is investing your regular net income that will grow to the required amount. Likewise, consider your retirement after which your regular income from the employer will cease. You will need an alternate source of income in the form of pension or interest or dividend. If you are not a government servant or you are not eligible for pension, you will have to create a corpus for yourself that will provide you necessary income when you grow old. If you work for the same employer long enough, you may be eligible for gratuity alongside any contributions to the provident fund scheme that will mature and come in handy. Nevertheless, you may fall short of the target corpus and need to invest additional amounts regularly to fill the gap. These are clear cases where money is directly involved to ensure a happy financial future.

Now, consider a case where a parent teaches children the value of money all through the latter's childhood and into their young-adulthood spanning around two decades inculcating the habit of spending money meaningfully, without splurging and better, investing for future needs. Being financially educated does not imply sacrificing happy moments or recreation that may cost some amount of money. It is about carefully yet spontaneously (from constant training) evaluating an expense and resisting impulse-buying to not regret later. This keeps a check on the family's spending and makes way for additional savings or investments as the need be. The family not only achieves financial independence over time but makes permanent scale up of their financial position for generations to come. There are families in this world where parents encourage children to actively undertake petty household chores and reward them, which teaches many lessons about the way of life in their later years. That reminds me a globally agreed fact that smart phones combined with 4G technology have been disruptive in spite of their greater contributions to the advancement of the (maniacal) modern man. Lifestyles of countless urban families have been disturbed as people glued their eyes to the small screens regardless of time that changed the circadian rhythms and sleep cycles, food habits, consequently inviting disorder of the digestive system, blood pressure, impaired sight, emotional instability, deterioration of human sentiment etc. to an already physical exercise deprived body. All these inevitably lead to depression and increased medical spending. If only people can reminisce their younger days and turn to their former habits of early wake-up, indulge in physical exercise, learn a skill, assume a hobby be it photography, art etc., worries directed on healthcare and related spending will significantly diminish, not to mention an increase in delightful mental health, energy, confidence and improved performance at workplace that will bring better opportunities and subsequently higher incomes.

I wish you just had not a sigh of relief hoping this discussion has come to an end. Well, financial planning is hardly the examples you have read above. Tax planning that includes assessing tax liability and knowing tax benefits allowed by the Income Tax Act and various other related laws; understanding various financial and non-financial risks in life and making suitable provisions should the risks arise; evaluating various financial products and investment strategies in relation to defined financial goals; creating alternate sources of income so as to not feel the heat should the present income breaks, creating an estate over long years and bequeathing it to the next generation properly; for a single parent (divorced/widowed/otherwise), having to raise the kids all by oneself while focusing on the career; measuring the impact of rising price levels on the future cash flows and adequacy of corpus created; acquiring new skills to stay in the competition and not become obsolete (and the list goes on and on and on) are all an integral part of a comprehensive financial planning process. The crux of all of this is that our financial decisions and actions ensure our hard-earned money works harder for us and help achieve our goals.

Life's Needs and Goals

In introduction and central idea, we have already seen what needs and goals are like. You also must have observed by now that I have been using the terms needs and goals most of the time together. So, are needs and goals not the same? There is a difference between the two. A need can be a goal, but a goal may not always be a need. A need is something that you must plan for, even if it means making provisions for it by sacrificing certain comforts today else, financially life will become difficult in the future. It is something that you cannot postpone or avoid or overlook. Conversely, a goal is usually a kind of wish or desire to enjoy/experience/achieve something that will bring personal satisfaction, comfort, and relaxation. Goals are what we can call a 'Wishlist'. Though in the present context I am differentiating between the two, you can objectify the word goal and attribute it to the term Need. It is like saying 'realizing that need is my goal'. In practice, it is important that you clearly see both separately because, in the initial stages of planning, prioritisation of needs and goals is critical. Inappropriate prioritisation caused by mistaking a goal for a need can make the plan messy and eventually force you to recreate it all over again. Let us start with needs.

Financial Needs

After reading the above description, if I ask you what is the most important need that comes to your mind that you must make first provisions for, what would you say? Take a moment and ponder. India has of late been in the forefront in terms of globally-acknowledged technical, scientific, and medical advancements that have reached even far flung rural areas through the expanse of the country. Yet, many age-old sentiments still linger in most families regardless of religion, income class, education, and geography. These sentiments have even put countless advisers behind the line for decades for the fear of losing business and clients which is why even today millions of families in India are not at all or inadequately insured to cover the most critical risk – Death. In the absence of adequate alternate income or other provisions and means of survival, death of a bread-earning family member throws the family into destitution, that might not put mere survival at the front but destroy the future of the next generation too. Unarguably, that puts taking cover from death risk, as the most important financial need to be addressed.

Do you want to guess what critical need you should plan for, next? This one is worse than the former but when we give it a serious thought, death risk comparatively is given priority over this. The second most important need one must plan for, is the risk of Disability. It is like a double-edged knife. On one side, the bread-earner has supported the family for a long time and now he cannot move a twig, let alone himself. On the other side, he becomes a burden on the family who cannot now feed themselves. A responsible individual who loves his family may prefer death to disability; such is the latter's curse. Besides, it is equally unpredictable and no less important than death.

Are you safe yet? Days are gone when you could have simply stayed home, enjoyed lavish estate, and prevented mishaps. Like I said, life is cruel. In the modern West, there is a saying about Karma that I wish I can quote. Despite all humanly efforts that can be put, one cannot escape the risk of falling terribly ill. That puts Terminal Illness in the third place on the list of most important needs to be addressed in the order of importance. Simply take the example of Cancer (not the Sun sign or Moon sign for astrological predictions but the disease). No one knows which part or organ of the body it will attack, how and when. All the disciplined things you do in your life and perfect lifestyle you maintain are not enough to prevent it. It can be breast cancer in women, prostate cancer in men, colon cancer, lung cancer, blood, brain, liver, oral, pancreatic, renal… how many can you avoid unless you just not feel god, but you are God himself (or herself)? I hope you have noticed that I have been talking about prevention, not the treatment for cure. Do you know how much it costs to cure such a terrible and critical illness? Do not you think a risk such as this needs priority planning?

If I have been successful in terrifying you with a streak of probable disasters that life can throw at us, half of my objective in authoring this book is achieved. Death parts us from life's atrocities but what if we are left with the risk of survival? Yes, living too long is a risk too. Over the years, individually and in groups I asked people how long they expect (not wish) to live and the figure ninety percent of the time never crossed seventy but occasionally seventy-five. My father has been talking about himself since he was fifty-five and he is seventy-two. So, when a client throws such an age-number at me, I am not shaken, but stirred to undertake the responsibility of educating. Say, I plan for my expenses (independent of children's contribution) for a life expectancy of seventy but blessed by the Almighty, I live to see ninety-five. I will exhaust entire corpus by seventy. How will I survive the next twenty-five years? Medical science has advanced so much that doctors will do anything to not merely keep us alive but healthy too. Thus, Longevity is a risk that needs protection through retirement planning.

Financial Goals

Once critical needs have been accommodated, you are at liberty to consider including various financial goals also in the plan. Similar as in the case of needs, goals also must be prioritised. This is necessary because, while developing the plan one or more goals may have to be compromised or if need be, eliminated too and it helps to know in advance which one to strike-off, as numerous calculations will not allow easy modifications and force reworking of the entire plan. Examples of financial goals can be – desiring to retire to a farmhouse in the country, upgrading a car once every few years or even better upgrade to a higher-end model, taking your spouse for a vacation on a cruise to the dream destination, creating a seed capital for your ward for establishing a business or profession after university and apprenticeship etc. You list of goals may never be limited but your means to achieve all those are. Hence, the need for prioritisation of goals!

Before we proceed and conclude this section, let us understand prioritisation better. Prioritisation need not be within the needs or goals categories. It can also be between the two. Take for instance the lastly mentioned goal above – creating a seed capital. As a rule, it is a goal but depending on the personal financial position and importance an individual attach to it, it can be categorised as a financial need. Likewise, let us draw a comparison between two needs viz. retirement pension and children higher education. Take a moment and reflect which is superior between the two. Some say children higher education is a priority while a few lay importance on making provisions for old age income and other needs first. In the present times, an adviser usually puts retirement planning over higher education and there is a valid reason to it from his (learned) perspective. With the support of a parent, a student can always acquire an educational loan to pursue the dream of higher education at a renowned university or elsewhere, but no financial institution whatsoever ever comes forward to lend money to the destitute merely to survive for decades on borrowed money. Of course, if the children are caring, responsible and financially supportive, in a civilisation and culture like India's the question of borrowing may not ever arise for the old-aged. But with changing times, the longevity of sentiments shrinks too without exceptions of culture and nationality. Financial planning is all about making provisions not merely for the foreseen but also for the unforeseen. What if children are incapable of lending financial support or lacks sentiment or separated from parents by geography or other compulsive reasons? Thus, while old age income and children higher education are needs by nature, when it comes to prioritisation, pension planning is preferred to the latter. Below is the writer's view of needs (ranked) and goals.

Financial Needs	Financial Goals
Life Insurance	Lavish Wedding
Disability Insurance	Business Setup
Critical Illness Insurance	Wealth Creation
Retirement Planning	Grand Vacation
Health Insurance	House Refurbishing
Children Higher Education	Gambling
Contingency Planning	Charity
Skill Development	Hobby
Debt Management...	Fly to the moon...

A hobby from the view of the plan should be something that demands substantial amount of money to pursue it but not something such as writing, sketching, karaoke, dancing etc., which involve learning those skills first, to convert it into a hobby.

Commanders of Planning

Why is financial planning so important? True, the goals are the drivers of planning but what makes planning them so carefully in advance, necessary? I see three factors. Even in the absence of these factors, planning for life's needs and goals is required but the three factors make it inevitable. Though I have not named them yet, I have already illustrated their need in the previous sections. The three factors are – Uncertainty, Inflation and Longevity.

Uncertainty

This is something in life that we cannot control. A goal where you know that you will need some money few years hence is something that you know for sure will come along and you can plan for it sufficiently in advance (unless you have change of plans enroute). But how would you know for sure that you will have an emergency or contract an illness or meet with an accident? You would not. These are called contingencies, not to be mistaken particularly as medical emergencies only. These form one side of uncertainty that you will encounter in your life at a micro level i.e. these uncertainties influence the life of a single individual or a family and will not affect others or the society. On the other side exist such uncertainties that affect a community or the economy and have a larger effect on the society, in some cases not impacting individual lives depending on personal financial positions. Such uncertainties can be, rise in prices due to supply and demand inequalities, decrease in the interest rate on our savings and deposits, withdrawal of subsidies by government on certain products, increase in taxes on income, goods and services, political events etc. We have no control over such macroeconomic causes. Alongside, difficult events such as job or income loss disturb the financial lives of individuals and families. All these uncertainties make planning in advance with a good foresight inevitable in the absence of which, life will financially become difficult, eventually making life quite unhappy.

The rich culture of India has not come to it over thousands of years but prevailed on this land since the very beginning, even before glorious civilisations rose and fell on other continents that separated and drifted away from the mainland; at least that is the theory most Indians grow up believing. There was a time when the joint family system used to be an inherent part of this land that is not seen anywhere else on the planet. As the saying 'birds of the same feather flock together' goes, families lived together and in harmony, headed by an elder or the active eldest. They had varying skill levels, occupational preferences, and earnings but they all contributed to the family financially and in other ways in their own capacity. Best, they were together and for one another – one for all and all for all. Times have changed (which is natural) but that is not what is sad. Everything changed in a matter of a mere hundred years and individuals of same blood could not stand the mere sight of a brother or a cousin or an uncle. Like the formation of continents, they parted into smaller, nuclear families and after generations of separation, though the formal greetings have started to bud among them again, they remained nuclear, alone and for themselves. Those that can fend for themselves are carrying on with only a sigh of sorry when someone closely related cannot. But tables can always turn either way. In either case, families with a single earning member encounter risks of making ends meet when bread-earners cannot manage their families' financial needs. My heart also bleeds often for those aged parents that are deserted by their grown-up children. Not merely to fill the gap at times but a second income always gives confidence and financial comfort to the family besides helping in meeting the financial needs without apprehensions. Such second income can come from two sources – one, salary or business income of another member in the family and the other, interest or dividend on investments, rent etc. Having both i.e. more than two sources of income including that of the main earning member, is more appreciable as in the present day, it is possible for both earning members in the family to lose jobs in overlapping periods.

Some may say that it is 'easier said than done' but I say different. If one is not affluent already either from heredity or nuptial or dexterity, one can yet strive to bring about a change in their lives on their own accord. I believe every individual is born with some skill that is sometimes dormant or forgotten due to compelling life situations or forced alternate occupations or mere lack of push from a motivating mentor. If all that is not appealing, for any educated or skilled individual that naturally possesses good sense, there should be something that he or she is drawn to or finds stimulating, be it art, music, photography, literature, blogging, teaching, collecting, travelling and what not.

When every external motivation fails, mere attraction to such a subject of interest can spark the drive to take the first step to success. If one is not sure even about that, one should seek counsel of an experienced financial planner or a professional consultant. All that said, a minimum, additional income is indispensable as a backup, should there be any contingency.

What are those contingencies that we are afraid, will befall us? Usually for those who are in private service, it can mean a gap in employment that can exist for a few months. Regardless of such a gap, one will have to pay for basic needs such as the insurance premiums, monthly rations, credit card and utility bills, children school fee etc. In the absence of a promised income, financial life will be thrown into utter chaos forcing the family to borrow for meeting immediate needs and lapsing insurance policies and the like, in the struggle to manage liabilities. It is always best not to challenge fate and ignore the risks because the moment you do and your policy lapses (or something of the sort), the need for hospitalisation due to accident or diagnosis or some unforeseen situation may make its way into the already hammered life, forcing you to pawn or sell any financial and fixed assets that you may have acquired until that moment. If not that, sometimes a close friend or someone in the family may come running for financial support in the short term and not being in a capacity to help despite earning handsomely (at least as it may seem to the needy) may feel real-bad. You should understand that these are not emergencies and particularly not medical, but contingencies. For medical emergencies, we shall make enough provisions through other means.

To address such contingencies, one must resolve to create a contingency fund during their hay days, that is highly liquid and risk-free. It is recommended that such a fund be created through one-time allocation if one's personal financial position permits or create the fund progressively over a few months but ideally not drag beyond twelve. A contingency fund must be refilled at the earliest possibilities after it has been dug into, or else the purpose of such a fund and its mention in this book and your carefully drafted financial plan is destroyed.

Inflation

In 1990, I remember our family buying milk for Rs. 5 a litre. In 2019, we are shelling out Rs. 50 a litre. That is a year-on-year rise of 8.50% over the last 28 years. In the mid-90s, minimum rate of autorickshaw travel costed Rs. 4. Today it is Rs. 12 i.e. a yearly growth of 4.90 % approximately. Similarly, getting a pair of clothes ironed used to cost Rs. 0.50 and today the same costs Rs. 14, a yearly rise of 15.60%. This is called Inflation – the rise in price levels. Some expenses rise at a higher rate than the average and some, lower. While planning, we usually go with the average rate across regular expenses and plan for the projected future expenses. Though it has nothing to do with inflation, that reminds me the average USD-INR exchange rate, which used to be Rs. 18 per dollar is today, trading at Rs. 70 per dollar. Compare inflation in some expenses in India, in the below image (rounded-off for general idea).

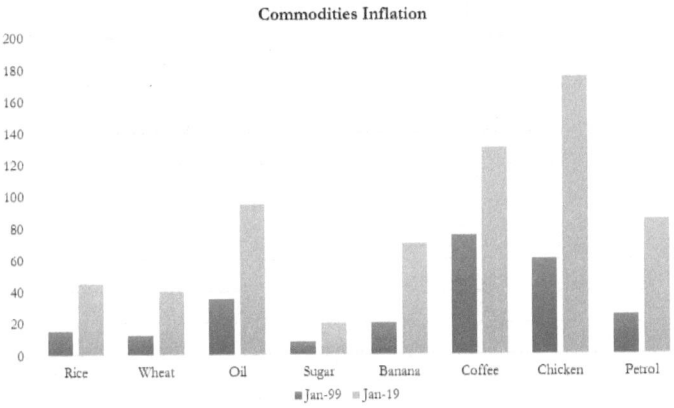

It is because of inflation that incomes appreciate over time. Imagine an individual who has an income of Rs. 50000 a month and a monthly expenditure of Rs. 20000. Suppose there is no inflation in any of the expenses and there is no change in the lifestyle either. The expenditure of Rs. 20000 will continue even after retirement. For 30 years i.e. from thirty to sixty, the individual saved Rs. 30000 a month and has life expectancy of 30 years after retirement. The 30000 per month savings the individual made will be enough during the post-retirement period to cover living expenses and other needs. Hence, there is no need for an increase in the income. Besides, investing or saving such surplus money every month gives more than needed.

Another care one must take while estimating future prices is that inflation is different for each category of expenditure. For example, inflation in food and household expenses can average out to say 6%, inflation in wedding expenses can be 8%, inflation in health care can be 10% and inflation in higher education such as management, medicine etc. can be 15% and so on. When the return on investment far exceeds the inflation rate, one may be able to achieve a goal within available means. However, when the inflation is higher and the spread between the return on investment and inflation is wide, or the inflation exceeds the return, the amount investible towards goals may increase by a huge percentage, often making it seem impossible to achieve. While we have compared inflation among various food expenses, let us see how higher education expenses can increase in the long term, at higher rates.

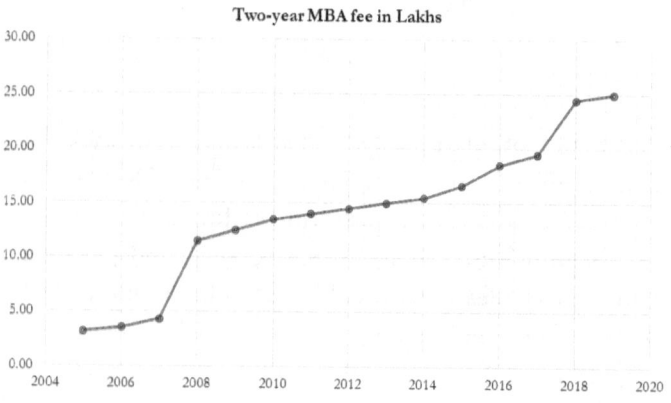

Two-year MBA fee in Lakhs

Nevertheless, one must be careful while working with percentages. Whenever I ask individuals in my meetings or presentations what they think the inflation rate is, while some say that RBI declared some percentage the previous week or the news said something, always to my surprise and content (that I have a subject and opportunity to speak for few extra minutes), I receive wild guesses from individuals, whose answers range from 4% to 15%. One must remember that percentages are not to be meddled with. In the long term, a deviation of mere 1% in inflation rate assumption can increase or decrease the future requirement of funds by 30% and a difference of 2% can change the estimates by 75%. Imagine someone assuming long-term inflation rate to be 5% while the actual average works out to 7%. That means, at present value if the expenses are Rs. 30000 per month, in old age, because of assuming lower inflation rate of only 5%, one will have to adjust with mere 30000 while actual expenses can be Rs. 52000. In the below image, see how actual expenses can be re unsuspectingly high at different inflation rates.

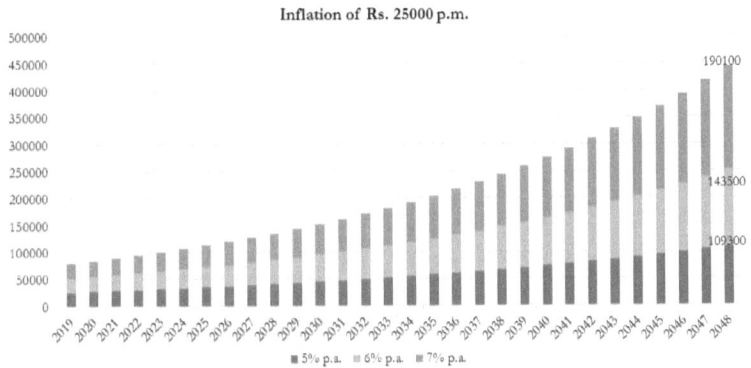

This effect of percentages applies to rates of return as well. Observe the below given two tables.

Amount	Inflation	Future Cost	Expected Return	Invest p.a.	Actual Return	Future Value	Deficit
5 Lakhs	6%	2870000	12%	10600	10%	1920000	950000
Inflation being same, 12% expected on 10600 p.a. but return turned out to be only 10% p.a.							

Amount	Expected Inflation	Future Cost	Expected Inflation	Actual Cost	Invest @ 12%	Invest @ 10%	Deficit
5 Lakhs	6%	2870000	8%	5030000	18600	27800	1660000
Expected a lower inflation rate and a higher return but bother turned out be opposites.							

Inflation rate being same, if return on investment is assumed to be higher than the actual average, one will end up with far lesser corpus in hand, when the goal is due, thereby destroying the relevance of the plan and fulfilment of its purpose. While one miscalculation is enough to destroy the plan, imagine making wrong assumptions regarding inflation and return rates together. Thus, Inflation becomes second vital reason to plan for financial needs and goals, while any percentage is critical.

Foundations of the Profession

The concept of financial planning made its ways to India about fourteen years ago and I have been associated with the profession since its nascent stages in the country. For anyone who has been in the profession all along, it has been a long time though not in general comparison to other professions. The industry has seen remarkable surge in its fame, suffered sluggishness and challenges from related professions within the financial services industry. Yet, persistent efforts of the members including the certificants helped its penetration into various branches such as share broking, insurance, mutual funds and banks and all groups are promoting the idea of advanced and methodical planning of personal finances among their clientele. Some organisations that were financially sound took to advising without a charge as they distributed their own and various third-party financial products while a few continued to offer impartial advice for a reasonable fee. Financial Planning, which was once an unrecognised profession lacking governmental support is today regulated, more organised, and acknowledged in India. Yet, I estimate that less than three percent of Indian households have exposure to structured comprehensive financial advice even that also, which some experts may argue, exaggerated. Irrespective of the argument, there is a dire need for professional personal financial advice of this nature in India, particularly for the untouched, isolated, and discriminated rural geography that is non-paying for the urban commercial entities. *Before you proceed, note that the next two sections viz. 'Board and Network' and 'Rules of the Profession' talk about the organisations that regulate financial planning profession in India, and the rules, standards and code of ethics set for the professionals. This has been included so that the reader, whether an individual seeking advice or a novice adviser, may understand what it means and takes to be a financial planner.*

Board and Network

The idea of financial planning had its genesis in USA as back as in 1973. By 1985 there were already an estimated ten thousand professionals. These were called the Certified Financial Planners (CFP), the certification that was conferred on those that met the education and experience eligibility criteria required by the program. In that year, with support from the Institute of Certified Financial Planners (a US membership group), a new organisation was set up that will own the CFP certification marks. Initially called the International Board of Standards and Practices for Certified Financial Planners Inc., it was renamed Certified Financial Planner Board of Standards Inc. (CFP Board) in 1994. After long years of domestic existence in the US, the idea of an international professional organisation sparked in 2002 and though the Financial Planning Standards Board (FPSB) was established in the year 2003 with John Carpenter as the Board Chairperson, the rights to CFP certification marks were acquired by FPSB in 2004 and that marked a new beginning to a truly global financial planning profession. I urge every student and practitioner to read the tenth anniversary book published by FPSB to understand what kind of passion, sincerity, dedication, vision, and hardships of remarkable people such as Tim Kochis, Elaine Bedel, Maureen Tsu, Noel Maye, and many others the profession has been built on. I advise even a regular reader or individual planning to employ the services of a financial planner to read the year book and understand that every CFP works for his clients with equal passion, integrity, and values. FPSB recommends three tenets to guide efforts to oversee and regulate the financial planning profession in a territory.

- Use of the title "financial planner" should be protected in law or regulation.
- Financial planners should be held to a fiduciary standard of care in law or regulation.
- Oversight of financial planners should be undertaken by a professional financial planning body.

Financial Planning Standards Board Ltd. (FPSB) defines financial planning as a "**process of developing strategies to help people manage their financial affairs to meet life goals**". In creating their recommendations and plans, financial planners may review all relevant aspects of a client's situation across a breadth of financial planning activities, including inter-relationships among often conflicting objectives.

The FPSB Council is a forum for financial planning organizations from around the world seeking to build awareness of the CERTIFIED FINANCIAL PLANNER marks and the profession of financial planning. The FPSB Council acts as an advisory and consultative body to FPSB's Board of Directors and includes delegates from each of the member organizations. FPSB member organizations are non-profit professional financial planning, membership and/or certification bodies that partner with FPSB to deliver CERTIFIED FINANCIAL PLANNER certification in a territory. FPSB and its member organizations (collectively, the FPSB network) collaborate to develop, promote, and enforce global CFP certification requirements and standards for financial planning. Currently, FPSB has member organizations in 26 territories that certify more than 175,000 individuals to use the CFP, CERTIFIED FINANCIAL PLANNER and CFP Mark marks. In 2019, the member organisations are present in United States, India, Australia, Austria, Brazil, Canada, Chinese Taipei, Colombia, France, Germany, Hong Kong, Indonesia, Ireland, Japan, Malaysia, New Zealand, China, Korea, Singapore, South Africa, Switzerland, Thailand, Netherlands, and the United Kingdom. Two associate members are from Israel and Turkey. (**Source: FPSB**)

Securities and Exchange Board of India

For years, other than that of FPSB, which is a recognised institution in the United States and its Indian affiliate, there has been no governmental regulation and supervision of financial planning education and professional practice in India though unofficially the Board, the Certification and the Profession were acknowledged and promoted collectively by various organisations in the financial services industry. Putting an end to the unspoken yet unsettled thoughts of the certificants and practitioners about their future, validity of the profession and its survival, in a landmark move in the year 2013, SEBI announced 'Securities and Exchange Board of India (Investment Advisers) Regulations, 2013 that were published in The Gazette of India on January 21, 2013 and came into force on the ninetieth day from the date of the publication. These regulations are primarily meant for financial advisers, preventing brokers, agents, distributors, consultants etc. in the financial services domain involved in selling of various financial products for commissions or incentives and misrepresenting themselves as advisers. The regulations also define the education, experience, and operational guidelines for registering and practicing as financial advisers – individual and corporate. A brief list of such regulations is given below for the reader's quick reference. A registered financial adviser shall be –

- ✓ A graduate in any discipline with at least five years of experience in financial advisory or a post-graduate in related subjects such as banking, commerce, economics, insurance etc.
- ✓ Certified in financial planning or investment advisory from National Institute of Securities Markets (NISM sponsored by SEBI) or NSE or BSE or the Financial Planning Standards Board or any other organisation or institution accredited by NISM.
- ✓ Act in a fiduciary capacity towards the clients, disclose all conflicts of interests as and when they arise and maintain arms-length relationship between advisory and other activities. An investment adviser

shall act honestly, fairly and in the best interests of its clients.
- ✓ and in the integrity of the market.
- ✓ Assess risk profile of the client by obtaining necessary information through a carefully designed, unambiguous and relevant questionnaire that is thoroughly assessed and communicated to the client for taking investment or financial decisions that are in line with the defined financial goals.
- ✓ The investment adviser shall ensure that fees charged to the clients is fair and reasonable. They shall not receive any fee, remuneration, incentive, consideration or income directly or indirectly from any other party whosoever in relation to the financial or investment advice given to the client, other than the client being advised i.e. the only income a registered adviser must have is the fee paid by his client for his advice and service and nothing else.
- ✓ An investment adviser shall have adequate procedure for expeditious grievance redressal. Client grievances pertaining to financial products in which investments have been made based on investment advice, shall fall within the purview of the regulator of such financial product. Any dispute between the investment adviser and his client may be resolved through arbitration or through Ombudsman authorized or appointed for the purpose by any regulatory authority, as applicable.
- ✓ An investment adviser shall maintain clients' records either in physical or electronic form and preserved for a minimum period of five years. Such records pertain to Know Your Client records of the

client; Risk profiling and risk assessment of the client; Suitability assessment of the advice being provided; Copies of agreements with clients, if any; Investment advice provided, whether written or oral; Rationale for arriving at investment advice, duly signed and dated; A register or record containing list of the clients, the date of advice, nature of the advice, the products or securities in which advice was rendered and fee, if any charged for such advice.

In the light of the point five mentioned right-above, I wonder if the reader or other individual in India will be willing to pay fee for the advice or not. Subsequent to above regulations, SEBI released a consultation paper and a discussion paper seeking opinions from various parties such as banks, insurance companies and mutual funds for amending the regulations, remove loop holes and further strengthen financial advisory practice in India in the interest of the clients or the general public that seek professional help. It has already been more than two years since the consultation paper was first released and the industry is anxiously waiting to see what decisions the regulator will take and how they will impact the industry and the careers of financial advisers.

Originally, the regulations prevented a single person or entity from involving in financial advisory and financial product distribution simultaneously. A distributor wanting to offer standalone advisory service too to the clients must do so through a separately identifiable department or division or a subsidiary only. Presently the regulator is considering withdrawing this relaxation, which means a corporate financial planner can either distribute financial products or provide fee-only service to the client but not both, either directly or indirectly. Likewise, an individual cannot register with SEBI as an adviser and then distribute financial products through any immediate family member.

I believe though it has been running with the sole objective of bringing transparency to the profession and ensure the financial interests of the advisors' clientele, the regulator gave the fact least thought that in India, people are willing to buy seemingly attractive financial products not understanding their practical relevance to their needs and goals while some yearn for pass-back of commissions and incentive income earned by distributors or if not anything else, Google and Bing for information on the internet and take uninformed decisions and be content or accept the consequences rather than pay for genuine, professional advice. Only time will tell how the industry will fare between such reluctant and careless public and enforcing regulator.

Planners & Networks

Today, there are around 1800 active Certified Financial Planners in India with the highest number 695 in the state of Maharashtra and a meagre 108 in the Telugu speaking two states – Andhra Pradesh and Telangana, for a combined population of 9 million. Considering eight members per family, that is at least one million families and only about a hundred active certificants all of whom may not be practicing, to cater to their financial planning needs. However, there are corporate financial planners too, couple of which I worked for some time. Their network, wider geographical presence, enough resources for marketing helped in serving a larger number of families than individual practitioners. Nevertheless, both play a crucial role in the development of the profession and financially disciplined society and the present number of willing professionals is very discouraging.

A financial planner usually charges a fee for the advice. The advice can be limited to a few select needs or goals, at times even a single need such as retirement planning or it can be comprehensive that addresses all the needs and goals of a family. Financial Planners can be categorised into two – fee based and fee only. [*Even after a decade of its active presence in India, financial planning has not gained the spread, as the advisers, to make a living, focused on selling financial products to their clients that are averse to paying a fee for the advice, but SEBI's regulations will change all that hence, hopefully. I am therefore compelled to cite examples and scenarios from other countries and not confine to India alone.*] A fee-based adviser typically receives commissions or incentives from distributing third-party financial products to his clients while he may provide financial planning advice freely to attract clients or to retain the existing ones in the name of value-additions. Conversely, a fee-only financial planner completely relies on the fee his clients pay for the plans or advice given to them, which makes it his/her only source of income. Fee-only financial planners act in fiduciary capacity towards their clients meaning, they act in the best interest of their clients as nothing else exists to motivate them to act otherwise. Some may not earn any commissions on third-party products but charge a percentage of the assets of their clients that they manage. The National Association of Personal Financial Advisors in the US believes that 'fee-only' is the most transparent and preferable model. Thanks to SEBI, today in India only a CFP or other qualified professionals that is registered with SEBI can alone call themselves Financial Planners or Financial Advisers but not the relationship managers, agents, brokers, distributors etc. associated with banks, stock brokers, insurance companies etc. This draws a line between the two sects and brings transparency because of which individuals and families seeking personal financial advice can decide whom to approach depending on their personal needs and preferences.

In the US, fee-only planners charge an average of US$ 180 to $240 per hour or $1800 to $2400 for a comprehensive financial plan. At an approximate currency exchange rate of INR70 for USD1, that calculates to an approximate average of Rs. 15000 per hour or Rs. 1.50 Lakh flat fee. Contrary to this math, in India, most corporate financial planners charge an average of Rs. 15000 for a comprehensive plan while there exists a wide range of Rs. 5000 to Rs. 15000 among individual financial planners. Nonetheless, fee usually charged in India is at least at a discount of ninety percent or more when compared to the scenario in US. Hourly fee system solely works on the mutual trust between the planner and his client as there can be no guarantee that a planner has worked certain number of hours on the client's plan. There can also not exist a system that can measure the time spent on the plan of a single client. Not for this reason necessarily but hourly-based fee model does not exist in India unlike in the US.

While in the US many non-governmental associations of financial planners exist such as the Garrett Planning Network (nation-wide network of hourly-based fee-only planners), in India, there have not been many or any for a long time. As the number of professionals that are attracted to the CFP profession increased over a period, an association by the name Network FP took shape, envisioned by Sadique Neelgund. After being dormant or not drawing much attention from financial planners for years after its establishment, over the last few years the association gained popularity among the adviser circles. Presently, Network FP conducts various continuing education programs, strives to create a thinktank, holds annual conferences for its members to help them grow their practice and provide quality advise to their clientele. Many organisations in the mutual funds and financial services segments recognise and support the initiatives of this association. The members of the association are not necessarily practicing financial planners.

Rules of the Profession

FPSB's Financial Planning Process consist of six steps that financial planning professionals use to consider all aspects of a client's financial situation when formulating financial planning strategies and making recommendations.

The practice of financial planning has not only grown significantly since its beginnings – it has had to change and adapt as the needs of consumers in various territories and regions change; as products, markets and regulatory/legislative environments evolve; and as financial planners develop new approaches and solutions to help their clients reach their financial and life goals. In response, FPSB has a global financial planning standards framework that includes:

- Competency and Education standards that describe the abilities, skills, attitudes, judgments, and knowledge that a financial planning professional draws on when working with clients in financial planning engagements;
- Ethics standards that provide guidance to financial planning professionals on appropriate and acceptable professional behaviour and judgment when delivering financial planning advice to clients, as well as responsibilities to the public, clients, colleagues, employers, and the profession;
- Practice standards that establish the level of practice expected of a financial planning professional engaged in the delivery of financial planning to a client; establish norms of professional practice and allow for consistent delivery of financial planning by financial planning professionals; and clarify the respective roles and responsibilities of financial planning professionals and their clients in financial planning engagements.

By adhering to ethical standards, financial planning professionals agree to provide financial planning in the interests of clients and with the highest ethical and professional standards and agree to uphold and promote the interests of the financial planning profession for the benefit of society. As part of their professional commitment, financial planning professionals should provide appropriate disclosures and agree to be bound by ethical standards when delivering financial planning to clients. FPSB has incorporated ethical behaviour and judgment, and compliance with ethical standards, into the global standards for CFP certification. To ensure these ethical obligations are understood, FPSB Members incorporate content on ethical standards, and their application, into territory-specific CFP certification standards. FPSB Members further adapt and enforce FPSB's ethical standards in their respective territories. FPSB expects that clients of financial planning professionals will benefit from a globally accepted set of ethical standards for financial planning professionals.

FPSB's Ethical Principles are statements expressing in general terms the ethical standards that financial planning professionals should adhere to in their professional activities; the comments following each Principle further explain the intent of the Principle. The Principles are aspirational and are intended to provide guidance for financial planning professionals on appropriate and acceptable professional behaviour. FPSB's Ethical Principles reflect financial planning professionals' recognition of their responsibilities to the public, clients, colleagues, and employers. The Principles guide the performance and activities of anyone involved in the practice of financial planning; the concept and intent of these Principles are adapted and enforced on CFP professionals by FPSB Members through territory-specific rules of professional conduct.

Principle 1 – Placing the client's interests first is a hallmark of professionalism, requiring the financial planning professional to act honestly and not place personal gain or advantage before the client's interests.

Principle 2 – Integrity requires honesty and candour in all professional matters. Financial planning professionals are placed impositions of trust by clients, and the ultimate source of that trust is the financial planning professional's personal integrity. Allowance can be made for legitimate differences of opinion, but integrity cannot co-exist with deceit or subordination of one's principles. Integrity requires the financial planning professional to observe both the letter and the spirit of the Code of Ethics.

Principle 3 – Objectivity requires intellectual honesty and impartiality. Regardless of the services delivered or the capacity in which a financial planning professional functions, objectivity requires financial planning professionals to ensure the integrity of their work, manage conflicts and exercise sound professional judgment.

Principle 4 – Fairness requires providing clients what they are due, owed or should expect from a professional relationship, and includes honesty and disclosure of material conflicts of interest. It involves managing one's own feelings, prejudices, and desires to achieve a proper balance of interests. Fairness is treating others in the same manner that you would want to be treated.

Principle 5 – Professionalism requires behaving with dignity and showing respect and courtesy to clients, fellow professionals, and others in business-related activities, and complying with appropriate rules, regulations, and professional requirements. Professionalism requires the financial planning professional, individually and in cooperation with peers, to enhance and maintain the profession's public image and its ability to serve the public interest.

Principle 6 – Competence requires attaining and maintaining an adequate level of abilities, skills, and knowledge in the provision of professional services. Competence also includes the wisdom to recognize one's own limitations and when consultation with other professionals is appropriate or referral to other professionals necessary. Competence requires the financial planning professional to make a continuing commitment to learning and professional improvement.

Principle 7 – Confidentiality requires client information to be protected and maintained in such a manner that allows access only to those who are authorized. A relationship of trust and confidence with the client can only be built on the understanding that the client's information will not be disclosed inappropriately.

Principle 8 – Diligence requires fulfilling professional commitments in a timely and thorough manner, and taking due care in planning, supervising, and delivering professional services.

CFP certification is the only globally recognized mark of professionalism for financial planners. When seeking objective, expert, and trusted financial planning advice, you should always look for the CFP mark. FPSB is an affiliate member of the International Organization of

Securities Commissions (IOSCO) and works with its network of member organizations at the national and regional levels to champion the interests of consumers and providers of financial planning advice. FPSB and its member organizations engage with regulators, legislators, and governments to have them recognize that financial planning is still an emerging professional practice around the world. Any regulatory or oversight models that are developed need to ensure the opportunity for growth of, and innovation within, the sector to better serve the public's needs.

Safeguarding the benefits

Before we plan, it is necessary that we evaluate and protect everything relevant to our existence. It may be fixed assets, financial assets, human life, health, friends, knowledge, occupation, and everything that is valuable and contributes to the financial wellbeing of a family directly or indirectly, either in the present or in the future. The idea of security arises because of uncertainty that is inherent in human life. An alternate to the word is, Risk. Just as science says that energy can neither be created not destroyed, so also risk is natural too and cannot be prevented or eliminated completely because Risk is inherently unpredictable. We encounter it in one form or another. The best that we can and must do is take necessary precautions to not invite it, not recklessly charge towards it and plan to recover from its after-affects.

When I talked about financial needs in the previous chapter, I narrated some risks that are prevalent in our lives and how we need to protect ourselves from those risks through insurance. If one's personal financial position is sound, he or she need not depend on insurance to protect the family's monetary interests but apportion various assets to come in handy when need be, without holding sentiments to the apportioned assets. An asset is something that has monetary value and income generation capability. Certain things that are freely and abundantly available to all cannot be insured. Likewise, assets whose monetary value is lost not because of some risk or peril but due to natural wear and tear cannot be insured. Assets that are damaged due to perils such as fire, theft, natural disasters, health hazards etc. can be insured. One must remember that by insuring, we are do not protect an asset but the benefit we derive from it. Human life is an asset too because of its income generation capacity, which is why we insure it. In this chapter, we are not talking about other risks that we might have overlooked in the previous chapter but understand the practical approach to address them.

Subject matter of solicitation

Understand, remember, constantly remind yourself and preach what I am about to say, just as you do and should, the Bhajagovindam of Adishankaracharya that is more of a universal philosophy than religious. The fundamental aspect of insurance is 'to make good the loss'. That means, in case of an unforeseen eventuality or accident or damage to an asset (including human life), insurance merely compensates the beneficiary (to whom insurance proceeds are intended to be paid) to the extent of pecuniary loss suffered. This is called the principle of Indemnity. Policies that insure human life are called Life Insurance plans and policies that insure absolutely everything else are Non-life or more commonly called General Insurance plans. Primarily, non-life insurance policies are based on the principle of indemnity. For example, a person who has a car that is valued at Rs. 5 Lakhs gets it insured for the full amount. Suppose the car meets with an accident and damage happens to the extent of Rs. 3 Lakhs. The insurer admits the claim up to Rs. 3 Lakhs only. Alternately, suppose the owner insures the car for Rs. 3 Lakhs only (wanting to save some premium) while the actual value is an estimated Rs. 5 Lakhs. In the eventual loss to the extent of say 1 Lakh, the insurance company pays only Rs. 60000 and not 1 Lakh. That is because, the owner insured the car only for 60% of the actual cost of the vehicle which, though not the intension, implies that the owner has financial ability to retain some risk and bear the loss to the extent of Rs. 2 Lakhs (difference between 5 Lakhs and 3 Lakhs). In continuation to the example, let us say the damage to the car has happened by the negligence of some other person. If the owner who suffered damage gets compensated by the insurer, he cannot again claim compensation from the party that has caused the damage. Such right to collect damages from the negligent party lies with the insurer only. This clause is called Subrogation. Imagine a scenario where the owner of the car insures his vehicle with two companies, for Rs. 5 Lakhs each. In case of accidental damage to the extent of say Rs. 3 Lakhs, the owner cannot claim Rs. 3 Lakhs from each insurer separately. If such a claim is admitted by both the insurers simultaneously, the owner will make a gain out of a loss, which contradicts the principle of indemnity and the concept of insurance itself. Hence, the total compensation from all insurers or policies cannot exceed the actual amount of loss incurred. This clause too is a continuation to Indemnity and applies for non-life insurance. It is called Contribution. If you are thinking how various companies will know that you have policies with others, do not worry. They have their ways. And, in the rarest of the rare case if they collectively pay the policyholder more than the indemnity, they will make sure they get back the extra claim. The policyholder should only worry about protecting his name and pride, by disclosing all material facts in utmost good faith so as not be shamed later when the dishonesty is revealed. Applicable to non-life insurance, there is one last principle that one must be aware of, before buying insurance. It is the principle of Proximate Cause. Sometimes, it is possible that a certain incident or accident occurs, but the asset or insured is not immediately damaged by this primary cause. The main accident may lead to a series of other events that eventually cause the damage. In such cases, even though the damage was eventually caused by some other incident, the insurer considers the main cause that led to such accidental damage. And, if such original cause has not been covered as one of the causes or perils under the insurance policy, the insurance company does not cover the damages and reject the claim.

Primarily, life insurance plans are of two types viz. Term Assurance and Pure Endowment. A term assurance plan admits the claim of the beneficiary and pays the proceeds only in case of death of the person whose life is insured, if the death occurs before the maturity of the policy i.e. if the policy holder survives until the maturity of the policy, he or she will not receive any money – a true form of insurance. Conversely, a pure endowment plan admits the claim of the policy holder or the beneficiary and pays the proceeds only if he or she survives until the maturity of the policy i.e. if the policy holder dies during the policy term, the family or dependents or legal heirs (or anyone else as the case may be) will not receive anything. Pure endowment plans no longer exist today. As one of my professors once aptly said, every life insurance policy other than term assurance is a combination of a death benefit and a survival benefit in different proportions. There is never anything great, admirable, or mesmerising about it. All through this book, wherever I use the word insurance, it implies making good the loss, unless I illustrate particularly how certain common endowment policies (not the pure ones) function.

Thus, by its very nature, insurance does not (and should not) involve profit or gain or return or interest or investment or saving or any other similar term that will give you money back or personal satisfaction. Before we talk about the doubts that have sparked in your mind about the policies you bought, let me clarify something about insurance plans. And, note that the words 'plan' and 'policy' are used here interchangeably and mean one and the same. For educational purposes, insurance is said to have existed for thousands of years across many civilisations. Let us not worry about history and the primitive methods of protection but understand its significance in the present. If the reader does not understand this part and accept the fact that insurance is solely a tool or mechanism for protecting the family's financial interests in an asset, he or she will never understand the spirit of financial planning itself and always treats it as an enforcement or a deferrable obligation or an avoidable expense that eats into the cashflows without a visible reward. You may read this Insurance section again and digest it if you please.

Understanding Insurance

An insurance policy is a contract between an Insurer and an Insured (policy holder). Though from the policy holder's point of view he or she is buying a policy from the insurer, technically it is considered as a proposal made by a person (proposer) to the insurer. When the insurer accepts the proposal and subsequently the proposer accepts the terms of the insurer and pays the premium, the proposal becomes a policy.

In insurance, risk is the uncertainty of something happening that may cause monetary loss. Let us understand through a widely-cited example. Imagine a town containing ten-thousand families. For reasons whatever, including lightning, power shortage, fire accident etc., every year ten random houses are damaged. Not knowing whose turn, it will be the next year, all the families come to an agreement. They pledge to share the loss of the ten families among the ten-thousand so that, whoever suffers the loss will get compensated. The average value of each property is estimated at Rs. 10 Lakhs. As the number of accidents in a year are ten, the total value of property at risk is Rs. 1 Crore. If all the ten-thousand families split the risk among themselves, each will have to contribute Rs. 1000. With as low as one thousand, a family is protected from a loss of Rs. 10 Lakhs every year. In ten years, in comparison to the value of the property, a family will have spent only a trifling percentage to take cover from the risk. That is how insurance works and it is based on the law of large numbers.

Suppose a family deliberately burns down their house to build a new and a stronger one and you come to know about it after they have been compensated! How would you feel? Or, imagine someone too over-confident and reluctant to share others risk and excluded themselves from the arrangement but unfortunately fate befalls the plight upon them. In a year, out of the ten houses that are damaged, the tenth belonged to the family that excluded itself from the risk-sharing agreement. However, with a trivial shortfall, adequate amount has been gathered to compensate damages of all the ten families. What do you say? Should the tenth house that did not share Rs. 1000 towards the collective fund be compensated to the extent of Rs. 10 Lakhs or not? If it were you, would you expect sympathy and help on humanitarian grounds? You may or you may not. But an insurance company certainly does not have the sentiments of a human being. If one is sympathetic among ten-thousand, it does not help. Besides, ten is the average, not the exact number of families estimated to suffer loss. In one year, it can be nine and in the next, it can be eleven. In an informal arrangement among the townsfolk, money saved in one year can help the eleventh family in the next, without having to increase the burden. Thus, insurance is not for situations where loss has already occurred. It is a protective measure taken to recover the pecuniary loss in case of possible or probable damage to an asset.

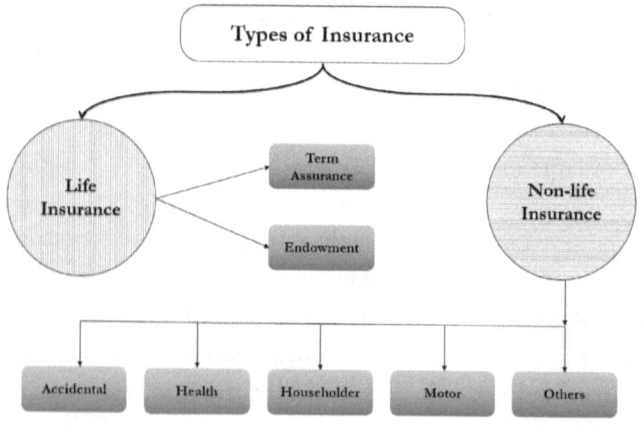

Today, two words viz. insurance and assurance are being used interchangeably as if no difference exist between them. However, from insurance point of view they are slightly different. Insurance deals with such risks that are not sure whether they will occur or not. For example, a driver of a vehicle may never meet with an accident whether he is careful or not, or a house may never catch fire due to short-circuit or some other reason. Even people who may pursue dangerous hobbies such as mountaineering, scuba diving, skiing etc. many never have an accident. The word 'insurance' is applied to cases such as these. Conversely, take the instance of death. We can never say that death may or may not occur. Death is certain. The only uncertainty about death is the time of its occurrence. In case of such uncertainties, the word 'assurance' is applied. That is why the term 'Term Assurance' was coined. On similar grounds, the risk cover in case of a life insurance policy is called Sum Assured while in the case of non-life insurance, it is called Sum Insured.

General Principles

As per Section 45 of The Insurance Laws (Amendment) Act, 2015, no policy will be called in question or repudiated on any ground including mis-statement of facts, after three years from the commencement of the policy. This is not the part where I bore you with voluminous texts on the laws and sections concerning insurance, but references are made to the general rules of insurance but only to the extent they are related directly to the insured and the policies. Let us go through a few important provisions that may help you further your understanding of insurance.

Surrender Value

Any insurer admits a claim only if the premium has been paid without any dues and the policy is in force. One cannot pay the premium after an event occurs and claim insurance compensation, which is why it is sensible to pay premiums on or before the scheduled due date. However, insurers usually allow Grace Period i.e. extra days to pay premiums beyond the actual due date. In cases of annual premium payments, the grace period is one month. In the absence of this provision, if the premium has not been paid on or before the due date, a policy goes into lapse. If the insured dies during the grace period without paying the premium due, insurers deduct the outstanding premiums from the claim proceeds. On the other hand, if the surviving policy holder fails to pay the premiums before the expiry of grace period, the policy lapses, which means the insurer is not obliged to admit the claim. A policy that has lapsed for reasons whatever may be revived subject to certain conditions. This is called Reinstatement of the policy laid down by the insurance company.

Depending on the type of the policy, the consequences of lapse may differ. Presently, let us see what happens in the case of an endowment plan. If at least three years premiums have been paid, a participating endowment policy accrues guaranteed surrender value i.e. if a policy has been in force and the policy holder wishes to terminate that policy before the actual maturity of the policy, certain amount is guaranteed. It is defined as 'thirty percent of all premiums paid, excluding the first-year premium'. For example, the yearly premium is Rs. 50000 for a twenty-year policy. If the policy is to be surrendered after paying premiums for five years, the guaranteed surrender value is calculated as below.

$$\text{Guaranteed Surrender Value} = ((50000*5) - 50000)*(30/100) = Rs.\ 60000$$

Let us be clear about this. If Rs. 2.50 Lakhs are paid as premiums in five years and you want to close the policy or surrender it, you will get a guaranteed amount of Rs. 60000. This does not include any bonuses. In any case, the amount received on surrender is always far inferior to the aggregate of premiums paid. If the endowment policy involves bonuses, the insurer may calculate and pay Special Surrender Value. Special surrender value is calculated as follows.

$$\text{Surrender Value Factor} * [(\text{Sum Assured} *(\text{No. of premiums paid/ payable})) + \text{Bonus}]$$

Suppose in the above example the sum assured is Rs. 5 Lakhs and a total bonus of Rs. 1 Lakh has been declared over five years. The hypothetical surrender value factor is 50%. The special surrender value calculates to Rs. 1.12 Lakh. Calculation can vary from insurer to insurer. The factor is derived based on the Paid-up Value and bonus. In short, paid-up value is a reduced sum assured proportionate to the premiums paid in relation to the total premium payment term.

The question is, whether one should surrender such an endowment policy at all or not. You have seen the impact above. However, there can be situations when you can go ahead and surrender a policy. Suppose you bought a policy with a term of twenty years. After four years of paying premiums, you come across an adviser who explains that it may be worthwhile to invest in some other financial product for long term, for higher return proportionate to the integral risk. In such a case, surrendering a policy even for a loss and diverting such periodic investments to a higher -return product that not only recovers the loss on account of surrender but also exceed the return maturity value of the original product may be more appreciable than continuing the policy for another sixteen years at a low rate. For example, Rs. 50000 per annum over five years in an endowment plan may give a surrender value of Rs. 1.25 Lakh. During the remaining fifteen years out of the twenty, if Rs. 50000 per annum is invested along with one-time surrender value at 12% per annum, the maturity value will be Rs. 28.22 Lakhs. Conversely, if the original investment is held for the entire twenty-year period, at an estimated return of 55, the maturity value will be Rs. 17.36 Lakhs. If this is done, surrendering is a better decision. But if out of twenty, already fifteen years premiums have been paid, surrendering may not be such a great idea. One must analyse the situation and take a decision carefully.

Rebate

For a very long time in India, insurance agents – be it the individuals or the corporate have been renowned for passing back the commissions to their clients or policy holders that they earned from selling insurance policies, either to earn, retain and increase their customer base as an agent or, earn rewards and awards as an employee of a corporate agent. This habit rubbed on the average person eventually became an epidemic that spread to other product categories such as small saving schemes of the post office, mutual funds, bonds and what not! Used to receiving or hearing about passing back of the hard-earned commission-income of the agents, a considerable number of proposers and investors pulled themselves so low that they insisted and demanded a rebate in the premiums in the nature of pass-back (a commonly used term). In the eagerness to receive rebate from whichever agent who offered it, the policy holder or the investor scarcely understood the true benefits of the policies and their relevance to their personal financial needs, while the agents, wounded by the attitude of their clients, mis-sold them such policies of the insurers that offered them highest commissions. After remarkable improvements in the financial services sector in India in the last decade, the vastness of the plague subsided but it is still prevalent among a paltry number of individuals in the urban and the rural societies. To curb this blot on the industry, the Act contained a provision that reads thus – *"No person shall allow or offer to allow, either directly or indirectly, as an inducement to any person to take or renew or continue an insurance in respect of any kind of risk relating to lives or property in India, any rebate of the whole or part of the commission payable or any rebate of the premium shown on the policy nor shall any person taking out or renewing or continuing a policy accept any rebate, except such rebate as may be allowed in accordance with the published prospectuses or tables of the insurer."* If an agent voluntarily offers a rebate, he may be penalised. But what if the proposer or client demands pass-back and the agent is compelled to oblige so as to not lose his business and a client? It is unfortunate that the Act did not put a condition to penalise the demanding prospects and clients of the agents, similar to the law that states, offering bribe is equally punishable as demanding and accepting it.

Claim Settlement Ratio

This term means serious business. But, due to its extensive usage by insurance agents in their meetings with their clients and prospects and the latter consequently habituated to the term and counting the figure as one of the decisive factors in narrowing-down insurance companies for buying a policy, it has lost its sheen. Sales persons and proposers alike usually look at claim settlement ratios before buying a policy. This happens in case of life insurance and particularly in the case of term insurance plans. If a company has a high ratio of say ninety-seven or ninety-five percent, it is considered a better choice, expecting the company to admit the claim whenever one is made. While there is no problem with the term itself or what it signifies, there is a great problem with agents and policyholders in understanding its true significance. In real, claim settlement ratio is calculated not merely for a specific category of policies but all types of policies together that are issued by an insurer viz. term assurance, endowment plan, money-back plan, whole-life plan, children plan etc. When an endowment policy matures (the term applied for, expires), the insurance company assumes that the policyholder is making a claim and that it is subsequently admitting the claim as if there would be a different outcome at maturity other than paying out the proceeds to the policy holder. Among all types of policies that a life insurance company sells, it is only the term assurance policy that has no savings element i.e. at maturity, the policyholder does not get anything in return. Note here that there are term policies that have an inbuilt feature – 'return of premium'. Such policies return all the premiums to the policy holders at maturity. Though such policies are called 'term with return of premium', having a savings element, they naturally fall under endowment category. Thus, the claim of every life insurance plan that has a savings element or maturity benefit associated, if not lapsed, will be admitted at maturity. Suppose, in a year, a life insurance company has received claims for one lakh policies. Among these, ninety-eight thousand are endowment policies that are completing their policy term and are due for compulsory pay-out and closure. The rest two-thousand are term assurance plans. Out of these two thousand, the insurer found inconsistencies and either withheld or rejected claims of five hundred policies. This takes the total number of claims settled to ninety-nine thousand five-hundred i.e. a claim settlement ratio of 99.50%! An amazing feat and credibility. But, let us take only the term assurance plans. Out of two-thousand claims, fifteen hundred have been admitted i.e. a claim settlement ratio of 75%. But the insurers and the regulator advertise and disclose only 99.50% as the claim-settlement ratio but not 75%. At least, I have never seen a break-up based on the policy type either in the IRDA annual reports or the websites of life insurers except for comparisons such as LIC-Private Sector; First year premium-Single premium-Renewal premium; Duration etc. Unaware of this fact, people usually look at claim settlement ratios and compare insurance companies to narrow-down their choices. The difference between claim settlement ratios like 97.50 and 96.50 is negligible in practical context and it does not mean that the policyholders will be doomed if they go with the insurer that has 96.50 ratio, or the insurer with 97.50 ratio showers lots of extra benefits on its policyholders. Even if one goes with the insurer that has 97.50% ratio, there is a possibility of 2.50% into which we may fall. One should understand the relevance and significance of this factor before attributing too much value or completely rejecting it or basing the decision on it.

Managing financial risks

In the present context, risk is the possibility or probability of incurring monetary loss or benefit resulting from damage to an asset, eventually leading to the expenditure for getting it repaired or replaced. By now, we are all ready to agree that risk is inherent in life. But, despite their uncertainty and unpredictability certain risks may be avoided and some may be controlled to a certain degree. But in all cases, insuring the risk is not the first, direct and only solution. There are diverse ways to handle risks. Take risk avoidance for example. I do not say one should avoid the possibility of meeting with an accident by never leaving the house or venture into sports for the fear of physical injury, no matter what. On the uncommon side, I may suggest that one should not run into the tide of the sea at the beach if one does not know how to swim or venture to climb a mountain the first time all alone but on a more practical note, I may suggest the example of using a stabilizer for expensive electronic equipment in house to prevent damage due to voltage fluctuations or, using 'earth' or 'ground' connection to avoid shocking electric shocks or even short-circuits at times leading to fire accidents. One must understand that risk avoidance is merely a measure, which may not fully eliminate the possibility of a peril that can occur in one form or the other. Risk avoidance reduces the possibility but, how do we reduce the volume of the loss in the event of a peril? For example, if one is driving a car, following traffic rules, obeying lights, and maintaining correct lane is risk avoidance while using air bags, seat belts, head protection etc. which, in the case of unescapable accident reduce the damage, not to the car but the human being. Likewise, maintaining healthy lifestyle through controlled diet and exercise is a risk avoidance measure while getting regular medical check-ups at least once a year or in case of frequent and recurring illnesses, which can identify an ailment that can be cured in its early stage is risk or loss reduction. Once the precautionary measures have been taken, it is time to address the risk through insurance or risk retention, also known as self-insurance. We already know what insurance is. Self-insurance is nothing but bearing the loss oneself using the specially created or available or borrowed funds. In case of self-insurance, as the funds are required to meet contingencies, they are usually invested in low-return yielding products for unknown periods. Alternately, if one insures the assets or risks for reasonable premiums, the funds may be invested in better products for higher returns. This is more significant when the funding for self-insurance require larger sums of money. There are risks that are related to investments, which are separately discussed in the next chapter.

Critical Insurances

In this section, we discuss about critical financial needs that must be covered through insurance, which we talked about in the previous chapter under 'life's needs and goals'. The discussion here is not about why the needs and insurances are critical but how to practically address these needs in life. These needs and insurances so indispensable that any impractical or vague assumptions can prove expensive in the long run. We shall also see whether certain insurance is necessary at all or not and in what condition, in such a way that it does not render the comprehensive financial plan useless. The critical risks and insurances that I discuss here are death, disability, and illness.

Death Risk

The risk of economic loss to the family in the event of death of the principal earning member or the head of the family is addressed through life insurance. But the question is, how much is a life worth? We all agree that unarguably every single life is equally invaluable. How then and for how much do we have to insure our lives? As it is difficult to value life itself, we must work our way around and instead of directly trying to find the suitable amount of insurance cover, calculate the probable pecuniary loss or the expected future contributions of the deceased to the family's financial needs, which is easier and more practical.

The foremost financial contribution of an earning member to the family is towards regular household needs or expenses. Secondly, he or she takes care of major financial needs such as education of children. But what is usually overlooked are the debts that the head of the family or the breadwinner got himself into. Who would know those liabilities except himself unless he shares with the family? If adequate arrangements are additionally not made to clear such liabilities, all the insurance policies that have been bought may not be enough to pay off the debts, let alone help the family achieve the goals or even worse, survive. Therefore, the third addition to calculate life insurance requirement is the outstanding financial liability. The aggregate amount thus arrived at, for which an individual buys a life insurance policy is called Human Life Value (HLV).

Most people that have ever met a life insurance agent or a relationship manager whether they bought a policy or not may have heard from them a thumb-rule that life insurance cover must be at least ten times the annual income or fifteen to twenty times the annual expenses and so on. One should understand that life is not so simple that we can manage it on thumb-rules. For example, in India, a caring father regardless of his financial position and income manages to provide for his child's education or girl's wedding (no gender bias here; a mere mention of the societal fact). If life insurance is bought based on thumb rules, critical needs such as these will never be addressed. Whether the reader is an individual seeking advice or a critic or an adviser himself, some may raise a question as to how an individual whose cashflow is unaccommodating, will be able to pay premium to sufficiently cover all the needs. A true, experienced, and concerned insurance agent or adviser would know well to educate and convince his client to buy insurance first even it if needs borrowing or pawning gold or some other asset before planning other needs. Let us take an example and then I will share a reference table to help the reader to quickly identify his approximate aggregate life insurance requirement.

HLV Illustration: Consider a married individual aged forty whose family's monthly expenses are Rs. 30000. His monthly income is Rs. 50000. The amount includes Rs. 5000 spent towards his personal care and commutation. His child is five whom he would like to see become a doctor. The child's higher education costs Rs. 50 Lakhs in today's value though the need is fifteen years away. He has about Rs. 5 Lakhs liabilities in the form of car loan. He is already paying premiums on policies worth Rs. 10 Lakhs risk cover. Let us calculate his life insurance requirement.

Ignoring his personal expenses, the man's contribution to the family is Rs. 3 Lakhs a year. Considering an average rise of 6% in the prices, by the time of his retirement age, say 60, the monthly expenses will have risen to Rs. 80000 i.e. in 20 years. If his family will have to survive in his absence (or more specifically, in absence of financial support from him), they will need such a lump sum amount, which if invested in risk-free avenues such as the bank fixed deposits will pay regular interest income of Rs. 25000 per month to begin with and go all the way up to Rs. 80000 per month over the next 20 years. That amount calculates to Rs. 55 Lakhs or at the current exchange rate, $78000 for a mere beginning income of Rs. 25000 or $355 a month. Now, are we not forgetting something? I will give you some time to think or see if any question pops up in your mind. A reader that has a financial bent of mind may even want to take up an argument if he gets a chance. I will answer your question in this very section later.

Coming to the education, the expenditure is expected to increase at an average rate of 10% a year. However, considering fifteen years of long time to the goal, the family may invest the insurance proceeds for a comparatively higher return of 12% per annum. To be able to meet the future cost of Rs. 2 Crores or $300000, an amount of Rs. 38 Lakhs or $55000 is required today. Summing up everything, the net insurance requirement is arrived at as follows.

Rs. 55 Lakhs + 38 Lakhs + 5 Lakhs − 10 Lakhs = Rs. 88 Lakhs or $125000 approximately

I do not hesitate to say that most insurance agents or relationship managers make quick calculations similar to thumb rules and assume insurance requirement to cover the education expenses as Rs. 50 Lakhs as if they will pay the premium on the difference of Rs. 12 Lakhs for the next 15 years. But a financial planner knows the value of the premium saved, its impact on future cashflows and realisation of other financial needs and goals and avoids the situation of being over-insured. Now, let us get back to the previously unanswered question that will address the position of being under-insured.

How will a dependent wife who has no income, survive in old age if an individual makes provision for her expenses only until his retirement age? Even though that was a mere example, it may not sound agreeable or digestible. So, let us rework the requirement. Suppose the wife will survive another 50 years i.e. 30 years after the retirement age of the individual (only for reference as we presume, he is deceased). The expenses of Rs. 25000 per month will have surged to Rs. 55 Lakhs per annum by age 85 of the wife. Do not relate this 55 Lakhs with the one in the above equation merely because they are same. This figure and that have no relation and must be understood not in figures but in the ideas. To meet the yearly expenses going all the way up to Rs. 55 Lakhs per year, a corpus or more specifically, a life insurance cover of Rs. 1.20 Crore is required. Thus, the above equation is updated as follows.

Rs. 1.20 Crore + 38 Lakhs + 5 Lakhs − 10 Lakhs = Rs. 1.53 Crore or $218000 approximately

An educated and experienced financial planner can think out of the box and further improve this calculation. Twenty years ago, interest rates on bank deposits used to be as high as 12% per annum. Over a period, commensurate with decreasing rate of price rise in India, a growing economy, interest rates have come down to 7% now, by the 2019, that too after a slight recovery 0.50%. As the economy strengthens, both the interest rates and the price rise rate will ease and may come down to 5% and 4% respectively. In such a scenario, a financial planner makes two separate calculations for the immediate long term and farther long term and arrive at a more practical and agreeable figure that is as precise as possible. In personal finance, knowing what to calculate is equally important as how to calculate.

Another idea also exists concerning life insurance policy term. The purpose of life insurance is to provide cover from the loss of income from the main earning member of the family. Most commonly, the earning of an individual continues only till a certain age, in some cases earlier than the average fifty-eight or sixty and some other times extended even till sixty-five and seldom, seventy. Throughout his earning phase, an individual constantly contributes to the financial needs of his family. His contributions naturally continue so long as his income continues, which is until his retirement age. Thus, it is logical that term insurance policies that may have been bought to cover entire life (Whole-life Plans) be discontinued after retirement as the purpose will have been met by then. Some may counter this idea and argue that if the individual can afford to continue paying the premiums after retirement, there is no harm in doing so as death is inevitable at some point in time though it may delay a little. This depends on the interest of the individual that is planning his finances with or without the support of an adviser subject to the allowance of his post-retirement cashflows.

Age of spouse	Years of need	Requirement based on current expenses		
		15000	25000	35000
25	65	68	113	158
30	60	65	108	152
35	55	62	103	145
40	50	59	98	137
45	45	55	92	128
50	40	51	85	119

In the above table, 'years of need' represents the number of years the spouse needs financial support, up to the age of ninety (life expectancy). The illustration has been prepared for monthly expenses of 15000, 25000 and 35000. Life insurance requirement given below monthly expenses is in rupees lakhs i.e. if for example the requirement is 119, it means 119 Lakhs or 1.19 Crore. Lastly, in the illustration, risk-free return on investment of life insurance claim proceeds is taken as 6% and inflation as 4% for the entire period.

MWP Act, 1874: We are already in concurrence that a life insurance plan is proposed by an individual primarily for the financial wellbeing of his family in his absence. However, if the individual leaves behind debts, the creditors may contest for a right over the insurance proceeds and in which case, the family for whom the insurance policy was intended in the first place will be left helpless and revert to the position as if no insurance policy ever existed. A great relief for this drawback has been provided in the Married Women Property Act, 1874. Section 6 of the act says *'a policy of insurance effected by any married man on his own life and expressed on the face of it to be for the benefit of his wife, or of his wife and children, or any of them, shall ensure and be deemed to be a trust for the benefit of his wife, or of his wife and children, or any of them according to the interests so expressed, and shall not, so long as any object of the trust remains, be subject to the control of the husband, or to his creditors, or form part of his estate.'* Admitted claim proceeds of a such a life insurance policy that is endorsed under this MWP Act, 1874 will assuredly go to the wife and/or children as defined in the endorsement. No other legal heir or person or creditors can, under any circumstances, claim a right or share in such proceeds.

There is another way to insure financial needs and goals such as higher education of children, wedding etc. Though it is about insurance, as it is a concept linked to a certain modern investment strategy that should be mentioned first, it is discussed in the next chapter, under Goal Planning.

Disability

One of the most underrated or inadequately measured critical risks in India is the risk of disability. Accident is one among the top major causes of death globally. Such a risk can be covered through disability insurance, again one of the cheapest forms of insurance. In case of life, risk of natural death increases with age. Hence, mortality premium is stepped up with age but levelled out into equated periodic amounts. Not just that. Premium of a thirty-year-old and a forty-year-old also differs in case of life insurance due to increased risk. Such is not the case with accidental disability as risk of accident affects everyone irrespective of age. Hence, the premium does not increase with age.

Imagine an individual who has a life insurance cover of Rs. 1 Crore. After a difficult day at work and a miserable argument with the boss, he leaves the office in an uncontrollable rage and rushes away on his bike. He suddenly feels his vision blurring and goes into deep sleep. Later he wakes up and finds himself on a hospital bed and tries to get down but cannot feel his legs that have been amputated. Imagine his plights – loss of job, disability, financial inability and what not. The 1 Crore life insurance he has will not help at all as the individual is still alive. In the absence of adequate assets to back the expenses and needs of a lifetime for the entire family, it is an unanswerable question as to how they will survive.

In case of death of an individual, life insurance considers expenses of only the dependants but not the bread-earner himself, but it is not so in this case. In case of disability, even the personal expenses of the disabled must be considered while calculating necessary insurance cover as regards the living expenses. While calculating life insurance, existing life insurance cover can and has to be adjusted to calculate net life insurance requirement. But as life insurance cover is insignificant in case of disability, existing life insurance policies must not be adjusted from disability insurance requirement. However, estimated cost of attaining critical financial needs such as children higher education are retained. Let us take the example from the life insurance illustration.

Illustration: Take the original expenditure of the family including the head as Rs. 30000 per month i.e. Rs. 3.60 Lakhs a year. In twenty years, these will have rose to Rs. 66 Lakhs and calculated for the life expectancy, the expenses will rise to Rs. 1.44 Crore or $206000. Substituting this in the equation for life insurance, the disability insurance cover is calculated as follows.

Rs. 1.44 Crore + 38 Lakhs + 5 Lakhs = Rs. 1.87 Crore or $267000 approximately

People believe at least in India if not elsewhere that mishaps occur in others' lives but not their own, not because there are usually watchful but simply because they believe so, until a disaster befalls them and they then they are denied insurance. We do not take cover from risks because they are certain to happen. We do so exactly for the opposite reason i.e. uncertainty.

In any accidental insurance plan, two main types of disabilities are mentioned viz. permanent total disability and permanent partial disability. Total disability means loss of at least two major organs such as limbs and eyes in any combination. Partial disability is the loss of any one major organ. In case of partial, the lump sum payment of claim proceeds is usually 50% of the total sum assured while in the case of total disability, 100% sum assured is paid. Total disablement has a variant – temporary i.e. the individual suffers total disablement of any two major organs but they disability is curable. In such a scenario, the policy does not pay the sum assured buy compensate the individual for the loss of income by making weekly or monthly payments for a limited period.

Health Care

I have not seen a hospital or a doctor in my life (not literally). Ever since my early childhood, I remember my father studying Homoeopathy as a hobby and giving the household and neighbourhood, medicines and I was never worried that he was not qualified. This is the legacy of the land of Telugu where beyond thirty years in the past, many educated were attracted to this medicine and practiced freely. This is not a promotion though, for this branch. Circumstances change with time and what was, will never always be, at lease to the extent that it concerns human life. Yoga may have become a craze in the present world, but it has been a way of life in India from time immemorial. Taking a positive view of life, maintaining a disciplined yet joyful lifestyle involving physical exhaustion and natural exercise helped humans until two generations before now in living healthy till the last breath. All that has changed now particularly in the concrete jungles (with continually sky-rocketing population and density per square kilometre) and owing to unavoidable progress of the economy that breached geographical boundaries. Eating habits, sudden surge in health-consciousness (such as cleansing body from inside with green tea), working odd hours in the nights in call centres even tiring out owls and bats in the competition to stay awake, living emotionless and insensitive life in the rush to climb the corporate ladder for promotions and accolades, deprivation of exposure to sunlight, consumption of over-the-counter non-prescription drugs like the cravings for sugar candy, immersion into the digital world of social networking, gaming and screen-time indifferent to the circadian rhythms, exceeding plastic pollution and greenhouse effects and many other changes in the likes of these had permanent effects on immune systems that even common illnesses are challenging the efficacy of tested and approved medications. Afterall, it is only natural that such lifestyles lead to hospitalisations and prolonged treatments beyond twenty-four hours. Scientific and technological advancements cannot be stopped or controlled nor the livelihoods of the modern age but how life must be lived given the free will of man, can be corrected for better. All those unspeakable, unheeded, and horrendous elements combined with the costs of healthcare going through the roof make buying health insurance inevitable not because it stands as a barrier to ailments but to obtain proper treatment.

Adequate health insurance cover can be chosen depending on the individual's and family's health history corresponding to the age and financial ability to pay premiums as it is more expensive than life and accidental insurances and increases at a higher rate with age than in the case of the former. While a majority consider a cover of Rs. 2 to 3 Lakhs enough, some that can afford higher premium prefer a cover of say Rs. 5 Lakhs to cover immediate family members who are limited to spouse, parents, and children. Such a policy is called a Floater Policy and comes in two variants – one, the cover for each family member is capped within the overall limit say, at Rs. 1.25 Lakh for each member in a family of four; and the second, each family member is covered for the collective or overall insurance cover of Rs. 5 Lakhs in this case. Maximum amount of health insurance cover one can buy can vary from insurer-to-insurer. Also note that the age of the oldest member in the group of family members that are being insured is considered for calculating the applicable group premium.

Beyond a certain age insurance companies insist on prior medical tests before accepting a proposal for health insurance and charge a bit of extra premium if they feel the risk is higher than normal. Thanks to the understanding modern times, competition and wisdom of insurers, even pre-existing ailments except congenital health issues are covered after a waiting period ranging from two to four years. There is also a general waiting period of one month. However, hospitalisation due to accident is given exemption from the waiting period. Most plans these days reimburse the expenses incurred on diagnosis and medicines up to a certain period before and after hospitalisation. In the brochures of the insurers, these feature as pre-hospitalisation and post-hospitalisation. Usually, for health insurance to apply, the patient must have been admitted in a recognised, minimum-beds hospital for more than twenty-four hours. But with technological advancements in the world of science, today, certain medical procedures do not take more than twenty-four hours. They are called day-care procedures and do not require more than 24 hours hospitalisation but there are certain exclusions to them. One must go through the list provided by the insurer before taking a decision.

Two other important clauses to lookout for, usually in higher sum insured health insurance plans are Co-pay and Deductible. In co-pay, the policy holder pays a fixed amount on every visit to the hospital above which the insurer pays irrespective of the expenditure incurred, up to the maximum limit of insurance. On the other hand, deductible is applicable for each policy year afresh. Suppose in a policy of 10 Lakhs the deductible is Rs. 3 Lakhs. On a visit to the hospital, the bill comes to Rs. 2 Lakhs. You will pay the entire Rs. 2 Lakhs. A few months later (in the same policy year) you again admit in the hospital and incur Rs. 3 Lakhs. This time you will pay only Rs. 1 Lakh and the insurance company pays the rest. For the rest of the year, if again you get hospitalised, the insurer will pay the entire amount as you already touched the yearly deductible of Rs. 3 Lakhs. But who gets hospitalised again and again in the same year, merely to make the insurance company pay their bills for their satisfaction? However, the deductible will start all over again the next policy year. Opting for co-pay or deductible usually offers a discount on the premium. Those that buy smaller insurance covers up to Rs. 5 Lakhs are advised to avoid these setbacks. Similarly, certain policies have sub-limits on expenses such as room rent, consumables etc. A new feature is trending among health insurance plans lately – coverage for non-allopathic treatments such as Ayurvedam, Homoeopathy, Unani, Naturopathy etc. One who has been used to consulting a qualified doctor of these medicines may claim such expenses under health insurance.

All that aside, there is one more question that some readers may feel unanswered. One may say that they have health insurance cover from their employer, be it the government or a public sector undertaking or a private entity or through Employee State Insurance (ESI). Before anything else, I urge such individuals to check the adequacy of insurance cover provided to them under the group policy and know the benefits such a policy offers. Second, particularly those serving in the private sector should give a considerable thought to purchasing a separate health insurance policy over and above the group insurance, at least for a minimal sum insured if not equal or higher. This protects the individual and the family in times when the employer cover is not available for reasons whatsoever.

Terminal Illness

If you can recollect, in the financial needs section of the previous chapter, I left the estimated costs for treating critical illnesses to your imagination but not abandoned you. I shall address them here. A terminal or critical illness is one, which usually leads to death after a stage of severity has been reached. Unless miraculously identified at an early stage, such a disease or ailment is incurable through regular treatment, medication and care in certain cases control the problem and prolongs the lifespan significantly. But it is a fact that Indians are disappointingly inactive at getting regular medical check-ups as a part of preventive healthcare. Raw translation of a Telugu saying is, 'like holding leaves after hands are burnt', which widely suits Indians (which I cannot say about other countries but believe it is the same everywhere).

In India, treating a critical illness is expensive for the domestic populace though some affluent nations find the costs comparatively economical. While actual costs may vary from one to another, all such ailments cost significant sums of money that a regular health insurance policy of three or five lakhs sum insured cannot address. Cost of treatments can range from ten lakhs to a crore on the higher end, but sometimes depend on the class of the hospital the patient is admitted into. The main feature of critical illness insurance is that upon first diagnosis, the insurer pays 50%

to 100% of the sum insured, depending on the stage of the illness without the obligation of first undergoing treatment or, cashless hospitalisation as in the case of regular health insurance. The most commonly covered critical illnesses are Stroke, Heart Attack, Bypass Surgery, Heart Valve Replacement, Multiple Sclerosis, Cancer, Kidney Failure, Paralysis, Parkinson, Alzheimer, Organ Transplantation, Bone Marrow, Brain Tumour, Blindness etc. subject to certain exclusions. Critical illness plans of insurers differ in inclusions i.e. an illness covered by one insurer may not be covered by another in their respective plans or vice-versa though not in entirety. I wish you remember what I said about Insurance in the second paragraph of that section regarding non-life insurance. Well, health insurance is a subject matter of general insurance and so as disability. Even though general insurance companies offer Mediclaim policies (health insurance), some insurers specialise in health insurance business but still come under the purview of non-life insurance. However, of late even life insurance companies are offering health insurance plans and critical illness plans. But such critical illness plans offered by life insurance companies may focus on one or select few illnesses only, such as cancer. Hence, comparing plans of various companies is critical.

Regardless of the type of insurance proposed to be bought, I advise the reader to do the following.

1. Know what is excluded under the policy and check its suitability for personal needs
2. Look for unnecessary features in policies before buying and avoid them if alternatives exist

3. Read the proposal form thoroughly and disclose all material facts compulsorily and honestly
4. Pay premiums compulsorily on or before the regular due date even if grace period exists
5. Never lapse or surrender an endowment policy unless you expect nothing back from it

Note that all policies including health insurance offered by life insurance companies have monthly and quarterly premium payment options too, in addition to annual. On the contrary, general and health insurance policies by non-life insurance companies allow only yearly premium payments.

Other Contingencies

All that we have discussed in this chapter yet are critical risks, which in the order of priority come first. However, there are other financial risks that we are exposed to. It is not that these that I shall explain in this section are insignificant, but they are not as devastating as the previous ones though in one or two instances they can be life-threatening. After accommodating all the critical financial needs but before making apportionments for financial goals, these are some other needs that we must address in the plan. Besides the two that I mention here, others such as marine insurance, public liability insurance, fiduciary etc. exist but they are not relevant to personal finance.

Householder Insurance

Ever since the dawn of civilisation in India thousands of years before the recorded history, thieving has been considered one, in a group of sixty-four remarkable arts or skills (do not ask me to name the rest). I say one does not believe it or perceive it so until they encounter it and suffer a grand experience such as a cousin of mine experienced recently or my father, a former general insurance professional did, about forty years ago. Some families that are financially well placed may secure their valuables such as jewels, gold, documents and what not in safes maintained by banks. But everything may not be deposited in safes. For example, valuables like expensive art, antique earthenware, collectibles, silverware etc. and common household items such as an expensive high-end smart phone, an ultra-high-definition 3D or curved television, a double-door refrigerator, an air conditioner, UPS etc. Some valuables can get stolen, some may catch fire, some may burnout due to voltage fluctuations or short-circuit etc. While safeguarding the valuables and maintaining electronics etc. with care is a protective measure, in the event of an unforeseen damage due to such hazards, to recover the loss of an asset such as these, one needs to insure them. This is where general insurance companies come in. They insure items as big as a building along with the compound wall and those that are as common as a pedal cycle and baggage for very reasonable premiums. Yet, Householders Policy remains the insurance that is most underestimated and unacknowledged by public and majority financial advisers alike. One thing that the reader must note is that the items are not insured at original price i.e. replaceable value. They are depreciated at standard rates at the time of renewal and insured at a reduced value only, which means that in case there is damage and the claim is admitted, the policy holder will only receive the current depreciated value but not the amount required to buy a latest item. Therefore, one may consider making provisions in the plan to purchase a new asset replacing the old due to accidental damage, so as to not dig into the funds allocated for other financial goals.

Liability Insurance

Here, we are talking about two distinct types – public liability and financial liability. Financial liability in this context means debts such as housing loan since they normally run into millions of rupees. This is linked to life insurance in that the life insurance requirement must be increased by the amount of outstanding housing loan taken by an individual. In the present times, it has become a practice for the lending banks and financial institutions to attach (through recommendation or involuntarily) a life insurance policy to the housing loan, with a sum assured that matches the housing loan amount. While a regular term assurance plan is taken for a fixed amount that continues throughout the selected term, in the case of loan-based policy, the sum assured decreases proportionate to the reducing balance of the loan i.e. the risk cover decreases every year by a certain percentage. However, premium does not change too. It is levelled for the entire term of the loan or the policy. Such policies also offer single premium payment option usually. Single premium payment is not always advisable (unless it is the only option) because in the event the borrower opts to prepay the outstanding balance and close the loan account, single premium once paid is not refundable even in part and will be a loss. Additionally, one must look out for any riders in the policies i.e. these loan-linked reducing balance term assurance policies may be sold along with additional risk covers such as the accidental disability insurance, critical illness covers etc. which have already been planned for, separately. Even if the premium on such additional benefits may not be pinching, unnecessarily shelling money on unwanted features is not an appreciable financial decision. Besides, benefits such as critical illness being subject matter of general insurance can be claimed only from one insurer, either the standalone policy bought separately or as a rider linked to this term plan. Is it necessary to complicate life and verify what the exclusions and conditions of the riders are, while trying to simplify and live a carefree financial life?

Public liability is the financial liability that arises out of the damage that drivers of passenger vehicles cause to others resulting in bodily injury or damage to another vehicle or asset. The Motor Vehicles Act, 1988 makes it compulsory to have insurance to cover such third-party damage. *No person shall use, except as a passenger, or cause or allow any other person to use, a motor vehicle in a public place, unless there is in force in relation to the use of the vehicle by that person or that other person, as the case may be, a policy of insurance.* This sort of liability is covered through third-party motor insurance. It even covers accidental death or injury caused to a third-party to an unlimited extent while in case of property damage caused by a four-wheeler, the amount of compensation will be Rs. 7.5 Lakhs and Rs. 1 Lakh in case of a two-wheeler. In accordance with a ruling of the honourable Supreme Court of India, the insurance regulator mandated all general insurance companies to compulsorily sell long-term third-party liability insurance policies of five-years for two-wheelers and three-years for four-wheelers in the passenger vehicle segment.

Realising needs and wants

Advisers often encounter clients that are not financially educated and yet, dismiss financial planning as mere investing or buying financial products, carrying themselves with an air of confidence acquired from meeting a few relationship managers or searching Google or Bing for information, not to ask right questions and understand but with mere intension of protesting the advisers and proving them wrong. The reader might have understood the crux of financial planning by now, after having read the first two chapters. In personal finance, unless an individual is impoverished, invariably planning for certain needs and goals involves making an investment. But the problem arises when a supposed adviser, inexperienced, without regard sucks it all up into an investment plan in the name of provisioning financial goals when critical needs are falling short or completely unaccommodated, throwing the financial security of the family into an abyss. However, if one is not open to hearing an adviser speak of investment products, how will a goal such as retirement planning be achieved, which needs significant investments usually over exceptionally long term? It is vital that financial security and financial goals are balanced, depending on the prevailing and projected future cashflows, and managing them in line with the priorities attributed to goals.

Notwithstanding the fact that financial risk management is profound, the study of investments is vast. In the planning parlance usually called Investment Planning, the subject can be quite confusing and daunting for a novice or anyone that is short of an experienced professional who studies most that is relevant to the world of investments whether related or suitable to an individual or family or not, only to be ready when a needy individual is encountered. Yet, the gap between the two can reduce if an individual who is desirous of planning himself or understanding what an adviser speaks, educates himself in the fundamentals of the subject. An individual need not study as elaborately as a trained adviser. For example, a professional usually studies how a deciding factor is arrived at or calculated, besides understanding what it means or how to read and apply it. Conversely, a commoner merely needs to understand the latter, since the former has already been worked out by experienced professionals. Nonetheless, the reader must not forget the tonnes of voluminous information crunched by the adviser (be it the laws or the dynamics of investing or the instructions/term & conditions/disclaimers in sight-challenging font and twisted language, that also carry an asterisk), in addition to understanding investor behaviours and drawing strategies for unique individual preferences acquired from meeting and advising a variety of clients.

Investment planning is about investing cashflows and apportioning assets to achieve the financial needs and goals. However, the job is not done once the investment is made. One needs to periodically review and rebalance one's investment portfolio to ensure that they continue to suit the related goals. I repeat, 'periodically', not constantly check, and fret over a decrease or enthuse over an increase in the value of the investments. Having said so much, selection of individual financial products is the last thing we do. There is much to do first. It is essential that every financial product that is bought be linked to a financial need and goal, at least wealth creation or else the purpose of careful and advanced planning is defeated. Prior to that, the amount that one needs to invest to achieve the goal has to be ascertained. And, before knowing the amount, one must know how much return is required to achieve the goal, given the available time and even before that, find out how much risk one is ready to take and before anything else, understand first what risk is.

Prerequisites of investing

<u>Debt Management</u>: A wise man once said, 'if you borrow, borrow so much that the worry is not yours to repay but the lender's, to collect it from you'. I do not know quoted that but that is just a metaphor, not intended to be experimented or practically executed. But, during my college days, my professor said that borrowing is no less than stealing. Trying to draw literal comparison, I did not interpret the statement and agree with him then but seeing people evade repayment of their liabilities or failing to repay out of their worsened financial positions and the lenders (corporate or individual creditors) having to write-off such loans as bad debts, clarified me the meaning over time.

Most credit card holders are confident before they get it that they will use it the right way – to make purchases and payoff before the due date, avoid interest and penalties, to acquire payback points or cashback, to improve or maintain their credit score etc. This lot includes those with prior experience of owning a card or the first-timers. However, only a handful are truly able to pull this off and maintain the card activity clean as they wished. But, along with the card comes attractive offers in colourful brochures or images to buy stuff in easy instalments, those items that did not cost much but one has been avoiding for saving money. Some resist the temptations but month after month, day after day, those offers continue to pour in by mail or email until one day the card-holder falls prey to one of those attractive schemes and makes a purchase. Remember King Julian in the film Madagascar 2 where he demonstrates offering sacrifice to the Gods? That is how the as the days go by the offers continue to come. Then the calculations start – my net income is xyz, my cash-outflow is abc and I still have a surplus of so-and-so that I can spend on credit card instalments. In no time, the entire limit on the card is exhausted and the things bought earlier begin to appear useless or less useful. One thinks a hundred times before buying life insurance or starting a mutual fund investment through the systematic route but never hesitates to fall into the debt trap. That is how it all begins.

In India, it is also not uncommon for working population below the age of thirty to be influenced and persuaded by their parents (or in-laws and spouse if married) into buying property on loan. After two or three years into the working phase after college, one is naturally swayed to apply for a housing loan and buy property. When one is determined, justifications supporting the decision pop up just like that. The property seems to be a great investment in a great locality, the loan instalment is a compulsory investment that otherwise is not invested anywhere, or if you cannot buy the property where you live, you can rent it so that it will cover the loan instalment, it provides tax benefit if not under Sec 80C, at least the interest is exempted under Sec 24 up to Rs. 2 Lakhs and if all those reasons do not convince your rational mind, then your colleague or friend who is your age or younger by a few months has already owned a great house. And suppose even that does not turn you on, your parents want to die in a house you or your family owns, not in a rented one where the owners might object for any rites. Consider a scenario where an individual has a monthly income of Rs. 1 Lakh (about $ 1400). The monthly expenses including existing rent and commutation amount to Rs. 45000. He goes for a loan that costs him Rs. 50000 per month but the removal of rent will bring the net burden to Rs. 35000 i.e. a total of Rs. 80000. Even though this is not very appreciable, at lease he has a surplus of Rs. 20000 to take protection from financial risks and make small investments. But, imagine the individual has an income of Rs. 30000 and his net outflow is Rs. 20000 a month. He goes for a loan that costs him monthly instalments of Rs. 15000. What will happen here? He starts cutting down the expenses to fill the shortfall of Rs. 5000. It does not end there. To accommodate the housing loan instalments, he is forced to stop all the investments and savings he was making out of the surplus of Rs. 10000. For a while, he continues to make partial withdrawals and when the savings are depleted, he begins to borrow within his circle as he is no longer eligible for additional loan owing to the already availed housing loan. Add the credit card situation to this which was acquired before the housing loan was availed and you will see a beautiful picture of debt, which is again not uncommon among the middle-class (upper or lower does not matter much). Check the below table illustrating the comparison between house property purchased through loan of Rs. 10 Lakhs (100% financed) and estimated instalments of Rs. 115800 per annum invested in securities for the term of the loan (20 years).

Year	Interest	20% Tax on Interest	Tax Invested	House Value	House + Tax	Emi Invested
1	16547	3442	3442	1000000	1003000	115800
2	18280	3802	7657	1100000	1108000	245000
3	20194	4200	12776	1210000	1223000	390000
4	22309	4640	18950	1331000	1350000	553000
5	24645	5126	26350	1464000	1490000	735000
6	27226	5663	35175	1610000	1645000	939000
7	30076	6256	45652	1771000	1817000	1167000
8	33226	6911	58041	1948000	2006000	1423000
9	36705	7635	72640	2143000	2216000	1710000
10	40548	8434	89791	2357000	2447000	2031000
11	44794	9317	109884	2593000	2703000	2391000
12	49485	10293	133363	2852000	2985000	2794000
13	54667	11371	160737	3137000	3298000	3245000
14	60391	12561	192586	3451000	3644000	3750000
15	66715	13877	229574	3796000	4026000	4316000
16	73701	15330	272452	4176000	4448000	4950000
17	81418	16935	322081	4594000	4916000	5660000
18	89944	18708	379439	5053000	5432000	6455000
19	99362	20667	445639	5558000	6004000	7345000
20	109766	22831	521948	6114000	6636000	8342000

In the above example, the individual is assumed to be in 20% tax bracket and the savings on account of interest on housing loan under Sec 24 has been calculated along with 4% cess and shown in column 3. In column 4, the tax saved is supposed to have been invested at 12% per annum in equity. Column 5 shows the growth or inflation in the value of house property purchased through loan. The property is expected to grow at a high rate of 10% per annum, compared to the general assumption of majority financial planners. The last column shows how the amounts of Rs. 115800 per annum meant for loan instalments are instead invested in equity at 12% per annum. By the end of the year 20, the savings in the form of exempted tax invested along with the future value of the property are valued at 66 Lakhs while the investment in equity accumulated to Rs. 83 Lakhs.

For someone, whose discretionary cashflow is positive (surplus after all outflows), measures can be taken by creating a contingency fund and investing calculated amounts to replace any of the existing items in the future be it car or household electronics. But how would someone already in a debt trap do that? For such individuals, it is always best to focus first on reducing the debt burden before thinking about any other goal or contingency. If one has a defaulted credit card outstanding, borrowing from friends and family to clear the dues can be a clever idea as such loan may have zero or extremely low interest rate. But if the card is active with used credit, priority must be given to clear that debt as the interest rate on credit card in India can be as high as 48% per annum. If not cleared sooner, small payments made towards credit card dues get adjusted towards only the interest part and the principal amount due will never get cleared. Be it work or getting out of debt trap, sometimes it may be wise to address one critical issue at a time unless situations demand otherwise. If one has multiple debts, more difficult ones such as the credit card must be addressed first. One should explore if personal loans and housing loans, which were taken at high interest rates can be transferred to some other lending bank or financial institution for a lower interest rate. In case of such balance transfer, one may not see great relief in the instalment amount, but the principal part of the instalment increases significantly, resulting in early closure of the loan.

Some people differentiate liabilities as good-debt and bad-debt. For example, housing loan is considered a good debt being an investment (that we already discussed) alongside education loan and others. We can agree that investment in education is a good thing but have differences in agreeing to buying property on loan. Similarly, some say that car is a depreciating asset and buying it on loan is a two-way loss – on one side it is an obligated cash-outflow without any income generation capacity like any investment and on the other side, the value of the asset depreciates constantly while it also suffers from deterioration of its condition, which is contrary to investment in property that can generate rental income while its value continues to appreciate over time. Thus, car loan and credit cards fall into the bad-debt category. Similar to financial planning, the solution to getting out of debt trap starts with budgeting.

Often, a question arises in the minds of borrowers whether they should foreclose a housing loan or continue it. If the return on investment is so high that it is more than the inflation rate specific to the property, one can altogether postpone the house purchase to a long-term future date and invest the assumed instalments in a suitable financial product for accumulating the corpus. On the other hand, some individuals explore the tax benefits they get on the interest part of the loan instalments. Here, two conditions must be considered – the interest rate on loan in comparison to the expected return on investment and the income tax bracket into which they fall. If someone is in the 20% tax slab for example and can claim exemption on the interest rate, considering the combined benefit of the property growth rate and the tax exemption benefit in relation to the expected return on investment, one can proceed with the housing loan and buy property. One can also consider making partial payments towards the outstanding principal of the housing loan to bring the interest part of instalments down to the exemption limit of Rs. 2 Lakhs per annum, if enough corpus is available but should note that the interest part of the instalments continues to fall month-by-month.

Budgeting: While it is undeniable that understanding our tolerance towards investment risk is one of the first things we do, budgeting is the foremost step in the process of planning for our financial needs and goals. Knowing the present cash inflows and outflows in detail is crucial. Without deriving the discretionary cashflow i.e. surplus or deficit after paying for all expenses, one would not know if the personal finances are hard or there are some fundamental flaws in the expenditure pattern, which if corrected, will help in setting right the financial position of the family. It is also necessary for to ascertain how much money is at one's disposal for allocating to various financial needs depending on the priority attributed. Budgeting is as simple as it is crucial. Fundamentally, it involves categorizing all monthly household expenses into various groups and sub-groups. The key to purposeful budgeting lies in its classification. Refer the sample table below.

EXPENSE	MONTHLY	ANNUAL
Rent and Maintenance	15000	180000
Household Expenditure	13000	156000
Commutation	2500	30000
Clothing and Accessories	1000	12000
Dependants Expenses	4500	54000
Miscellaneous Expenses	14000	168000
Total Cash Outflow	50000	600000

It may seem rational to you but just give it a thought. What does commutation imply? Is there only one straight expenditure that falls under it? What are dependants' expenses and the miscellaneous? The above kind of table hides various expenses and does not fulfil the true purpose of budgeting. The expenditure chart must be more elaborate than this. Compare the above chart with the next one.

EXPENSE	SUBSET	MONTHLY	ANNUAL
Household Expenditure		28000	180000
	- Rent and Maintenance	15000	72000
	- Groceries/ Ration	6000	72000
	- Utilities / Bills	3500	42000
	- Maids / Servants	2500	30000
	- Personal Care	1000	12000

		2500	30000
Commutation	- Maintenance	250	3000
	- Petrol or Diesel	1500	18000
	- Insurance Premium	250	3000
	- Public Transport	500	6000
Clothing and Accessories		1000	12000
Dependants Expenses		4500	54000
	- Children Education	1000	12000
	- Parents Healthcare	1500	18000
	- Petty Expenses	500	6000
	- Pet Maintenance	1500	18000
Miscellaneous Expenses		14000	168000
	- Entertainment	1000	12000
	- Eating out	1500	18000
	- Presents	1000	12000
	- Vacation	5000	60000
	- Travelling	3000	36000
	- Charity	1000	12000

Is this table not self-explanatory? You know how much you spend on recreation, vacation, commutation etc. There are families and individuals who earn significantly more than their needs but wonder where all the money goes and how, despite their higher income, they gradually go penniless as they month-end gets closer and closer, desperate for their next salary credit to their bank accounts. Such situations arise mostly due to impulse buying. For example, you may be taking a stroll at the city centre or go to a mall with some friends. Something beautiful or attractive catches your eye or you may overcome with pride as your companions go on a shopping spree and you end up buying that, disregarding your wallet fill. While momentarily budgeting helps in critically reviewing one's spending habits, constant maintenance of a detailed book of accounts helps in data crunching, identifying spending patterns, frequency, size of expenditure etc. and might even help in estimating inflation rate at micro level at the time of reviewing the plan. The above table only a sample and one can be as creative as they wish to be. One can add expenses such as vehicle loan instalment, home loan instalment, ongoing health insurance premium etc. Alternately, insurance premiums may be excluded so as to identify the actual cashflow and if there is any surplus, review the existing policies based on prioritisation and if need be, surrender the existing policies and route the money to a different priority.

INCOME	MONTHLY	ANNUAL
Salary – Self	35000	420000
Salary – Spouse	20000	240000
Interest on Fixed Deposit	7000	84000
House Rent	8000	96000
Professional Income	15000	180000
Agricultural Income	5000	60000
Total Cash Inflow	90000	1080000

Whatever are the needs and goals, after adjusting the expenses in the previous table with the above cash inflow, there is a surplus of Rs. 40000 a month that can be apportioned suitably across insurance, investment, and liability products. Knowing how much net cashflow is available is equally important as finding how much planning for each need and goal costs. This is what I meant by budgeting.

Investment Risks

Remember the first thing I said in the section on Insurance in the previous chapter? Well, read and apply that here, again. 'Risk' is not to be feared. It is not bad by itself but depending on our actions and circumstances, it is wrongly perceived as bad or good. If you research, I mean explore internet through search engines, you may find a variety of investment risks such as business or default risk, market risk, interest rate risk, reinvestment risk, currency risk so on and so forth (though I can mention another dozen perplexing names merely for the sake of doing it and making it impossible for you to ascertain whether they all concern you or you should ignore some or all of them). You may still choose to read elsewhere and understand them but for larger audience, I will resist adding up words and simplify it for practical purposes.

Risk is of two types. One, you invest some money expecting either interest or dividend income or, expecting cumulative growth in the value of the investment. In this case, either the interest or principal amount is defaulted, or the principal value goes down by a percentage. The possibility of either depends on the type of investment one has invested in. The other, you invest some money in a product expecting it to grow by say 10.25% per year over the next ten years.

After 10 years, when you calculated the actual return (which fluctuates a lot between, due to inherent volatility), is measured as 9.75% growth. That means, for example if you invested Rs. 1 Lakh today and expect Rs. 2.65 Lakhs (an increase in value by 165%), you ended up with Rs. 2.53 Lakhs. In this case neither you suffered loss in the form of principal erosion nor is the decrease in profit so devastating that your goals are at stake.

These are the two fundamental risks that should concern an individual while investing for achievement of financial goals, particularly the long-term ones. No other risk that you may read about, can be controlled. The best thing one can do is, adopt such strategies that will neutralise these risks to a great extent if not eliminate them, though some theories suppose that holding an investment for a significant term may eliminate the risk too. Hence, reading about other types of investment risks or sweating over them is impractical, unless the objective is to obtain abundant knowledge and profess. Risks such as interest rate risk and reinvestment risk fall into this category that must be managed through strategic investment planning, if the investment portfolio is large and contains significant amounts in various asset classes.

Risk Tolerance

In investments, it is necessary to first settle if you have the willingness to assume the second of the two risks I mentioned above. Theoretically, risk profiling has gained popularity among the modern group of advisers and investors alike. However, the practical application varies to a great extent. When the subject of discussion is investment, risk profiling helps us in understanding the ability and willingness to take risk. Whether you take an investment decision yourself or implement the advice of a professional without rightly understanding your appetite or tolerance for risk, the outcome will be a grave and lasting experience. Usually, professionals try to understand the risk profile of their clients through a set of questions. Understanding risk profile in practical sense is what defines the success of a retirement or investment plan. When we sum up the risk profiling questionnaires designed and followed by advisers across geographies, we find that the following list of questions are commonly used. If we observe the entire process of financial planning, repeating some of these questions in the questionnaire may appear inapt when they are already available in some other form or document.

Let me exemplify some typical questions. One, 'what is your age' or 'what age group do you fall in?' Surprisingly, you see this in the questionnaire, after you already shared your date of birth in the data collection form, in the personal and family details section. If ever you see this question in the risk-profiling questionnaire, know that your age, no matter what, will be a deciding factor in determining your tolerance towards risk. The argument here is, one may be young but unwilling to risk their hard-earned money, investing in risky financial instruments. But it is of no concern or little concern to the adviser because, if you are within the specific age bracket, the adviser assumes and the questionnaire implies that you are a risk taker, even if you are shouting through a hundred amplifiers that you are not, simply because the risk-profiler is pre-designed, which the adviser cannot modify or unwilling to tailor it for the sake of a single client. Likewise, if you are an elderly person (to be specific, pre-retiree or retired), the adviser and the questionnaire impose conservative attitude to your investment choices and strategy though you are dying to take risk whether or not to achieve critical financial needs but for wealth creation, knowing all the consequences of investing in high risk investments at your age. I do not see any other reason for including 'Age' in the risk analysis process? Two, 'what's your income' or 'what is your income range? Again, you already disclosed your various sources of income in the income & expenses section of the data collection form or will do so shortly, but you still have to answer this question. Why is your income so important in defining your risk profile? Let us say a person earns just Rs. 20000 a month. After all the expenses and outflows, the person has a meagre Rs. 2000 a month at disposal i.e. 10% of the income. Now, the important thing to observe here is that, Rs. 2000 a month may not be enough to create adequate retirement corpus for maintaining similar life style after retirement which means, the person will have to seek higher rate of return in the long term, though it means taking higher risk. But what if the risk profiling questionnaire assumes that, since the person has less money to invest, whatever is available must be secured by investing in minimal risk investments? The person will end up with far less than what he will need and eventually, he will have to compromise on his already compromised lifestyle in old age. On the other hand, a person earning Rs. 50000 a month, after spending for household expenses and loan instalments, is left with Rs. 10000 a month i.e. 20% of income. Contrary to the general perception, if the person wishes to live a simpler lifestyle after retirement and cut down his expenses, Rs. 10000 a month may be more than enough to accumulate the required monies by retirement even at a conservative rate of return.

But the risk profiling questionnaire may assume higher risk tolerance level for the individual with higher income and suggests higher allocation to risky asset classes. In the long term, this will result in many times more than the required monies. Of course, there is no harm in that, if the individual understands the risk, its impact in the long-term and desires to create extra wealth beyond the need for retirement, but the risk profiler may not assume that.

That means, where higher rate of return is required, it has been ignored leaving the person with a huge gap in old age cashflows and where risk-free rate of return or slightly higher is enough, unwanted higher rate has been arranged. So, should risk profiling be based on income (earning capacity) or should it be based on the need (future lifestyle expenses)? If it is the latter, is not the question irrelevant and more likely dangerous? If you ever see this question, ask the advisor for explanation as to how the question is relevant or how the information is used to understand the risk profile. Is it as explained above or based on irrelevant point system?

You are financially responsible for how many persons? (Or) Have you any dependants? This question may have an extension, asking you not to include those persons that can be supported by your spouse's income. First, it must be remembered that in India, predominantly financial planning is done for the male earning member of the family, even if the wife is earning, in exceptional cases, for a single parent on unmarried individual's family. So, when the above question is asked, if it is being put to a man, it does not consider the probability of the spouse discontinuing work in the absence of her husband. I do not imply that this is always so, but the question does not give it a thought. Besides, if the individual's life insurance requirement is being calculated, ignoring spouse's income is logical but how is it relevant in the risk profiler? Second, how is it important that you have so many members in your household depending on you financially? That the financial plan simply needs is the expenditure incurred on these family members collectively. In addition to the expenses, the plan also focuses on various financial needs and goals no matter what they are and how many dependants the individual has. So, what exactly is this question doing in the risk profiling process? If you have only one dependant, the risk profiler may assume that you can take substantial risk, giving you a suitable score for that question. And, if you have more dependants say three or four or even more, naturally the score will be such that your risk tolerance is considered as conservative. You may have considerable discretionary cashflow to provide for the needs of the family but that is insignificant to the questionnaire.

How much loss can you tolerate pertaining to your investments? You may not see the exact question, but you certainly will see its variations. You are usually given options to choose from and they are like – 'I'm willing to take up to x% of loss in the capital', 'I can bear loss up to x% but not more than that', 'I don't mind if I lose money' etc. Now, what kind of person invests his hard-earned money with the objective of losing it? Did you ever make an investment and wished to make a loss or least, did not care if you lost it? If one must incur loss or if one needs to be ready to bear the loss, why invest at all? Is it not to achieve financial needs that we are doing such an elaborate and advanced planning? Investments can be structured and allocated in such a way that, when we apportion them towards various needs and goals depending on the time horizon, the risk associated with them can be considerably minimized, provided the portfolio is periodically reviewed. Further, remember that unless you sell for a loss, you do not actually incur it. It is merely notional or unrealised. Sometimes it really baffles me when professionals – individual or corporate, well-educated, and experienced, put irrelevant questions to their clients. We have seen some such questions above. Just to help you understand the height of this, I will take you through a separate set below.

Let us say, to the statement 'even if it means extremely high returns, I do not want any loss in my portfolio', you answered 'I strongly agree'. The next question that is posed to you may read like 'I want to be financially cautious', 'I earlier invested in risky products and profited', I am willing to bear short term losses for long term investments', 'I can take financial risk' etc. Even after making it quite clear that you do not want any risk in the portfolio, you are asked to respond to these insignificant statements or questions because, if you skip any question, the score will not be appropriate and if the correct risk profile cannot be identified as per the pre-defined questions, the advisor will not know what to do, since the questionnaire is a standard one that is set by his employer or some other professional for him to blindly follow. It is best to rephrase the question in a way that it removes ambiguity and other possibilities.

Some advisors go as far as asking you what you will do if an investment you made declines in value over a certain period. Will you panic and sell everything even for a loss? (Or) Will you sell some and keep the rest? (Or) Will you call it an opportunity to buy more, cheaply? It also will not be a stretch to imagine some asking you how you think the market will perform in the near to medium term. Relevant it may seem, but it is not. Let me explain. For a moment, let us assume you are averse to investment portfolio risk. You never invested in risky financial instruments and you do not understand what amount and what kind of risk is associated with various financial instruments. If educated and explained well, you may be willing to go for these risky products but with conditions like 'long term', 'not more than x %' etc. And the adviser too may eventually do so. But anyway, you will have to answer these questions. Remember that when you understand the risk associated with the investment, your view of the investment and your responses in the questionnaire may change. First, if the adviser wants to go by your choice (particularly when you do not have a clue about a certain type of product), why do you need him – a professional? Second, you also do not need an advisor if you will have to decide what to do when an investment is not performing well as it is expected to. Third, if your adviser is going to explain you and help you understand that will alter your response and attitude towards a particular asset type, the above question is simply irrelevant. It is not just irrelevant but a serious flaw in risk profiling. So, if your adviser does not educate you (if you are not already) before you answer the above questions, well, the entire process is a sheer waste.

Depending on your responses to these kinds of questions, scores or points are assigned and you will be categorised as 'Conservative', 'Moderate' or 'Aggressive' investor or anything in-between and an asset allocation (we will discuss about this in detail later) and strategy is decided and imposed on you through the so-called carefully designed and defined process. Usually the reason for this kind of extraneous method is it that the adviser is excited and has overlooked the true significance of the questions included in the questionnaire or it is the obsession to standardise the process that the adviser did not care for relevance of the questions. Or, it is simply the urge to show-off and mesmerise clients that they are following well-laid methods and processes. It can be anything and I do not know either why it is so. It is not the case with just one or two. Be it an independent advisor or a reputed, corporate financial advisor, it is the same everywhere except for a trifling number of exceptional professionals.

Practical approach

Now, if I tell you that if you do not want to take risk, the risk-free rate of return is 6% and at this rate you will have to invest 10000 every month to create the required retirement corpus of say 1 Crore and since, you can invest only 6000 a month, you will have to trim your expenses in old age to the extent of 40% (which is not small) but, if you invest in somewhat riskier product that yields better return than 6% in which case risk associated with it in the long term will be considerably minimised and you will be able to make 1 Crore, will you take my advice or not? Let us suppose you are willing to go with a higher risk product. Are you basing the product selection (or asset allocation) on your attitude, knowledge, and experience or, on the need for better rate of return to achieve your retirement corpus? Is not it the latter? Risk profiling and asset allocation take different forms in different situations and one needs to adopt a practical approach to achieve one's goals successfully.

The purpose of risk profiling is to understand the orientation of an individual towards investment risk and choices based on his past experiences if there are any, and knowledge. Also, usually one invests in a financial product just because a colleague or a friend did or, develops aversion to a category of investments because a friend or relative or a colleague lost a good sum investing in that (whom one may consider as the guru of investments or at least well experienced, if not a professional). We tend to forget that the one who lost is only experienced in bearing losses and making gains occasionally (might be meagre too) but not an expert or a professional. Another probability is that you read something about a product in a newspaper or heard an expert disagreeing with it on a business news channel and decided not to go with it or vote for it. So, if I say, with a return of 12% from a high risk investment you will be able to achieve your target of 100, with 9% return at moderate risk you will make 85 and with 6% return at low risk you will make 70, you can decide whether you want to go with high risk and high return investment or choose a low return investment and compromise on the cost of the goal or need i.e. you can decide if you want to spend 100 or go with 85 or be content with 70 on a particular need. If you want to cut down your expenses to 70, is not it obvious what your risk profile is?

All the above factors must be individually and collectively given due thought in the overall understanding of the risk profile of an individual. The initial questions we saw regarding age, income etc. do not actually define one's ability to take risk. In its Investment Adviser Regulations, SEBI mandated that for the purpose of giving investment advice, the adviser must gather information such as age, income, objectives, risk appetite etc. but not plainly mandated that such collection of information should be considered to determine the risk profile of the client. But it did say that the process must include assessment of a client's willingness and ability to take a hit on capital reduction. If the adviser uses a questionnaire or a tool, it must not be vague, misleading, confusing, and complex. The questions and answers must be straight, interpreted appropriately and not attribute unjustified weight to selective answers.

Asset Classification

It is said that the success of any investment portfolio is dependent on ideal asset allocation and not on the individual products we invest in. Such is the importance of asset allocation in an investment plan. All asset classes are different in terms of Risk, Return, Liquidity, Taxability, Time Horizon, and various other parameters, and they must be studied thoroughly to understand and quantify the said parameters. While some investors argue that no investment beats real estate or land, majority of the financial advisors and financial planners globally say different. In fact, in the long term, no investment or asset class can beat equity in terms of return. But it is not easy to have a ripe fruit in your hand without toiling and thus goes the famous saying that 'risk and return are directly proportional' meaning, higher the risk, higher the return.

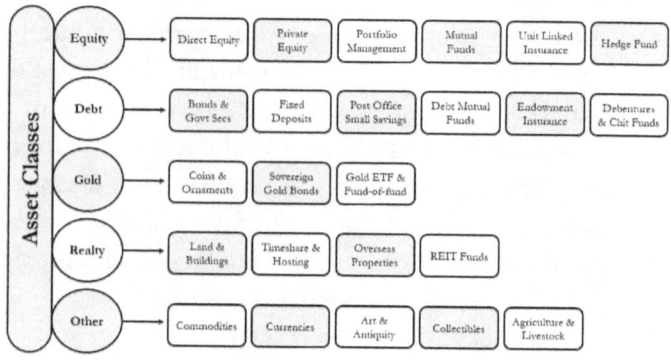

Equity, Debt, Gold and Realty are the most common asset classes for majority investors. While Equity is a high-risk asset class, Debt is comparatively, in general sense, less risky but seldom risk-free. Some advisers choose to call Debt as 'Bonds' or 'Fixed Income' but using those terms seemingly limit the diversity of the asset class. Some even go to the extent of treating 'Cash' as an asset class. The number of products that fall under the Debt category far exceed those that go under Equity, making it more complicated (arguable and opinion of some experts) to manage. Gold on the other hand is a favourite of every household in India, unarguably. Let us understand these individually. For simplicity, let us say, after understanding your risk profile well, you settled with an asset allocation containing three asset classes viz. equity, debt, and gold. Say, you are required to put say, 60% in equity, 30% in debt and 10% in gold. That means if you must invest Rs. 10000 every month, Rs. 6000 must go to equity, Rs. 3000 into debt and Rs. 1000 into gold. However, the real trouble is in understanding what equity exactly means and what debt stands for. When I told you to invest

6000 a month in equity, what does that imply? Which exact product you should invest in?

Equity

Whole books can be written, that too in many volumes, on Equity. I am not discussing all that here. In the world of investments, equity refers to investing in, or buying equity shares of a company, generally listed on stock exchanges such as the National Stock Exchange (NSE) and the Bombay Stock Exchange (BSE) though modes of One can invest in equity in the primary market when a company makes an Initial Public Offering (IPO) or buy in the secondary market. Returns from equity come in the form of capital appreciation i.e. growth in the share price. There can also be occasional dividend, bonus, and rights issues, which contribute to the overall return or percentage gain on the investment. Being very volatile, equity is considered as a high-risk asset class. Hence, except for risk-tolerant and educated traders, equity is always recommended for long term, meaning five years but at least three years. This is not a regulation or characteristic of equity investments but a general advice, advocated by investment managers. The periods attributed for long term and short term however differ in the case of income tax rules, which are defined by law and discussed in the chapter on 'Taxing Social Responsibilities'.

Investment in equity can be made in diverse ways such as Equity Shares, Equity-oriented Mutual Funds, Unit Linked Insurance Plans, Private Equity Funds, and Portfolio Management Service. Investment in any of these usually goes into equity shares of various companies, whether listed or not. Unarguably, if there is one thing that every person through the length and breadth of the country, whether knowledgeable or not, talks about, barring few other subjects such as politics, movies, and sports, in the context of this book, it is the share market or 'equity'. It will not be an exaggeration if I say that when two educated individuals sit for a discussion, stock exchanges and equity markets naturally creep in one way or the other. Just imagine how many brokers, distributors, researchers by the name of technical and fundamental analysts are offering tips and recommendations sometimes on a minute-to-minute basis to their clients and prospects to attract them into the business of trading. There are as many model portfolios as the numbers of advisors in the country. Like the saying, which goes thus - 'no two doctors prescribe the same medicine', no two model portfolios are alike. Coincidentally, there can be similarities between any two model portfolios but, for reasons unknown, the reasons for similarity (i.e. for including or excluding a scrip) between those are always different or sometimes even contradictory. After comparing all these, we can deduce that there is no hard-and-fast rule to creating a model portfolio so long it is rational and supported by agreeable research. Anyone can do it by carefully following certain principles. Before we go any further, let me clear one thing. Though I may say a thing or two about investing directly in equity shares or throw light on certain technical terminology, I may not suggest or give you methods to doing that. What I shall be taking you through is the right way to choosing an equity-oriented investment that is managed by a fund manager (which is not you or me). It can be a mutual fund, or a unit linked insurance plan, a portfolio management service, or a private equity fund. Even if one is reluctant to invest in managed funds such as mutual funds and portfolio management service or unit linked plans and prefer direct equity to the former, I strongly recommend seeking advice from a qualified and experienced professional.

Debt

Debt, which I already mentioned, is more diverse than equity in terms of products that fall under it. Some of the debt products are Bank Deposits, Corporate Fixed Deposits, Non-Convertible Debentures, Debt Mutual Funds, Public Provident Fund, Post Office Small Savings Schemes, Endowment Policies from life insurance companies etc. Some professionals brusquely reject to categorise certain products such as the public provident fund or an endowment policy as Debt. But if the underlying products directly or indirectly involve one party lending the money and another borrowing, and if we are investing in such products, I say they tantamount to Debt. It is more complicated than equity. Despite all that we discussed in the previous section, equity may sometimes seem simple to invest. From within, the blue-chip and large-cap category, identify sectors that are evergreen like FMCG, Banking, Pharma, Power etc., invest in those for long term, and sleep over those. I am not exactly advocating this style of investing but what I am saying is that the probability of earning desired return in the long term cannot be overruled in this style of investing too. Some time back, a mutual fund expert casually pointed that in the period that passed then, if one blindfolded put their finger on any scrip and held the investment through the passed phase, one would have earned exceptional returns regardless of the fundamentals of the company. But debt is not like that. Too many product categories, economic scenarios, interest rates, trading in case of certain kinds of products etc. makes this simple asset class, complicated. While I threw some light on suggested products in the section 'notable products' we shall discuss here bonds and debt mutual funds etc.

Debt literally means liability or money owed. In investments too, it means the same. In debt products, though product structure and design vary, eventually, one party lends money and the other party borrows. Putting it simply, as you are investing money, you are technically lending money and, directly or indirectly, the money you invest (lend) is borrowed by one or more parties. This is true in case of every debt product including endowment insurance plans, debt mutual funds, bonds etc. You do not need to worry about managing so many borrowers because, like in an equity-oriented mutual fund, usually experts take care of the job unless you are directly investing in products like plain vanilla bonds and non-convertible debentures, corporate fixed deposit schemes etc. The following are some issues usually taken care of by the fund manager, in products like endowment plans and debt mutual funds.

- Who to lend the monies received from the investors?
- For how long should the money be lent?
- For what purposes will the money lent be used?
- What is the credibility and creditworthiness of the borrower?
- Are the returns in the form of interest payment or capital appreciation or both?
- What interest rate must be asked or expected?
- What is the probability of interest rates going up once the money is lent?

That sounds simple, does it not? But there are few other things you should understand about debt. Like in equity, in debt too are many categories of funds such as long term, short term, etc. So, which is ideal for you? In short, I can tell you to start a systematic investment plan in a long-term debt fund or a short-term debt fund and invest every month into it until you the goal is achieved. But, as I know from experience that there is always the danger of an uneducated investor being wrongly guided or influenced into taking personally unfavourable investment decisions, let us learn a little more.

<u>Bonds</u>: Simply put, a bond is a fixed-income security. Buying a bond means lending certain amount of money to a borrower for an initially agreed period during which, the lender i.e. the buyer of bond receives usually fixed interest payments semi-annually or annually. The rate at which interest is paid is called Coupon Rate. Bonds are usually issued by governments, corporations, municipalities and large organizations or business entities to raise monies for meeting their project and business requirements. They require a large lump sum amount to invest and provide an alternative source of income. What if you are young and have lump sum monies to invest? You can consider buying a bond and reinvest the interest receipts regularly in equity or debt. Anyway, that is only a saying and investing in bonds or equity needs analysing personal financial requirements first that we discussed earlier.

You might have heard that 'bond prices fall when interest rates rise and vice versa'. Do you know why is that so or how that happens? Well, let us say I purchased a bond that offers an interest rate of 8% p.a. If you make an investment of 1 Lakh, you are paid interest of 8000 at the end of the year. Shortly after buying the bond, let us say I need money. Luckily, a friend agrees to buy the bond from me for 101000/-. What will he earn at the end of one year? He will receive 1.08 Lakh, which includes interest and the base principal. Since he paid 1.01 Lakh to me, his net interest is only 7000/- or 7%. So, what happened here? When the interest rate was 8%, the bond price was 1 Lakh. When 10100 was paid towards the bond price, interest dropped to 7% i.e. when interest rate fell, bond price increased and when interest rate was high, bond price was low (100000 instead of 101000).

How do you know what the right price for a bond is or what price you should pay for a bond? Valuation of a bond depends on the 'required rate of return' also called the discount rate. You must decide how much interest you need and whether that rate is before or after adjusting for tax. If a bond is offering 9% interest and you fall in the 20% tax slab, the net rate after tax will be 7.15%. Are you okay with this net return? But remember, if no other guaranteed instrument in the market is offering similar or better return, then you may consider going ahead with this. Again, you must be careful about the reinvestment risk. That means, when this instrument matures, the interest rates may be low and you will have to wait till the interest rates rise, keeping your money idle. Let us take an example to understand this better. A bond that has a face value of 1000 is offering 8% per annum for 10 years. Let us say you need a minimum return of 10% to achieve your goal. So, what price should you pay for this bond so that you will not lose because of low interest or coupon payments? To keep it simple, let us assume that interest is paid annually. The maximum price you should pay for the bond of 1000 face value in the example is Rs. 877. One must be cautious while buying bonds in the secondary market (that have already been bought by some other investor in the primary market). One needs to keep in mind, the yield to maturity, the price payable, liquidity and post-tax returns on the investment one can make.

Debt Funds: Equity mutual funds invest in equity shares of companies. But where do debt funds invest? Just like equity funds, there are various categories of debt funds such as long-term debt funds, short term debt funds, bond funds, gilt funds etc. Depending on the adopted strategy, maturity of the underlying investment and other factors, the category may differ. However, most debt funds usually have similar underlying product types such as Bonds, Debentures, Non-convertible Debentures (NCD), Government Securities etc. Schemes categorised as Liquid funds falling within the purview of debt invest in products such as Certificates of Deposits and Commercial Papers too. By whatever name they are called and whatever features and conditions they may have, they are all one and the same at the core – the investors' money is lent to various borrowers. Thus, what is important is the credibility and creditworthiness of the borrower to repay interest and principal as promised. Besides critically understanding the fundamentals of various investments, fund managers also consider ratings given for these underlying individual instruments by various Credit Rating Agencies such as CRISIL, CARE, ICRA etc. For example, the credit ratings issued by CRISIL range from 'AAA' (highest safety) and go all the way down to 'D' (default). Sometimes, a plus (+) or minus (-) may be added to these ratings. One should look at the underlying portfolio and the ratings of the securities too and satisfy themselves about the safety if they are risk averse, and the risk if they prefer active management. A thorough fundamental analysis of a company may also shed light on the quality of its papers.

The best thing about personal finance is that when you understand it through illustrations and examples, you will learn it like a charm. So, I again take you through an example. Let us say, I want to start a 'fee-based' financial planning company. I go to my bank and ask for a loan of 50 Lakhs. Unfortunately, the bank has a reserve of only 35 Lakhs. But, instead of driving me away, they issue certificate of deposit. To whom you ask? Not to me of course. I do not want papers and certificates. I want money. So, the bank has relationship with other financial institutions and business houses in the industry. The bank goes to those friends and says, "the fixed deposit rate is 9% but I will pay you 9.5% if you can help me with 15 Lakhs immediately". Investors jump and take that certificate of deposit and lend 15 Lakhs to the bank for an additional 0.5% interest. Now that it has 50 Lakhs, my bank calls me and says, "The normal lending rate is 10.50% but owing to higher risk and liquidity-crunch, we can fund you at 11%. Since no other bank or financial institution is ready to lend me the required money (that is the risk), I am ready to pay extra to anyone who is ready to lend me. So, what have you understood from this? That CDs offer better rate of return than the normal deposit rate prevailing in the market. But, can you directly get that extra rate of return? No. CDs & CPs are not available for individual or retail investors. But, if you still want to benefit from these, the best way is through a debt mutual fund, that is managed by an expert. The interest rates are not that high though, as taken in the example. Why should I approach a bank? Why cannot I raise the money from the market directly where I could get the funding at a lesser rate?

Simply, the reason is, I do not have enough reputation and goodwill to go out and get the money I need. If a blue-chip company asks for funds, you may see long queues in front of their offices. But it is not the same with everyone. Hence, the banks play the role of a mediator and fund us through CD. If you could raise the money like a blue-chip, then the same instrument is called Commercial Paper. Once you are comfortable with the aggregate percentage allocation to each security type i.e. all bonds together, all debentures together, all CDs together etc., you should verify credit rating of the products offered by the respective institutions. And the last thing that remains is, select a long term or short term or another debt fund carefully and invest in it in lump sum or through SIP, more of which is discussed in the next section of the chapter.

Experts suggest that one should invest in long term debt funds when interest rates are falling. Sounds good, but why? Let us take an example. Unexpected rains in the state destroyed the paddy and wheat crops over Lakhs of hectares, which led to a shortfall in the stock. You expect the price of these two commodities to rise sharply in the coming few months. What will you do? Buy the products in copious quantities and store in your house for future (or long term), don't you? Similarly, when interest rates are expected to fall soon, one should invest in long term debt products because the monies can be locked at high interest rates for a long time, without your having to worry about the probable fall in interest rates. Alternatively, when you expect the interest rates to rise or reverse, you invest in short term bond funds so that your monies will be readily available because of the shorter duration to maturity, when the interest rates peak. When it comes to debt mutual funds, whether short term or long term, the most important thing you should check for is the portfolio of the underlying assets in which the fund manager invested. The quality of the papers and the instruments both play key roles in achieving the expected return on the investment. Remember that when interest rates are falling, it is good to invest and lock your monies for the long term through long-term debt funds and adopt the opposite strategy in case of short-term debt funds.

Gold

Gold can be bought in the form of jewellery, coins, bars, or gold exchange traded funds, gold fund of funds or e-gold or through any scheme offered by gold shops. If Gold was purchased in Oct-2008 and held for 5 years i.e. till Oct-2013, the return would be 14.77%. If it was bought for an average of Rs. 29600 in 2013, at the beginning of 2019, with the price being 28800, the five-year return on gold calculates to -2.60%. If the same is calculated for longer period say last 30 years i.e. 1988 to 2018, the compounded growth rate calculates to 7.68% per annum, assuming gold was bought only once in three decades i.e. 30 years ago. Globally, advisors suggest that allocation to gold be maintained at 5%-7% of the total portfolio. In any case, the maximum allocation to gold shall not exceed 10%. There is another theory that did rounds in the advisor circle some time back according to which, if people were buying a dozen of apples 500 years ago and paid in gold (say, 0.15 gram), even today, if they have to pay in gold they have to shell out similar quantity i.e. 1gm Gold = 3000 and 1dz Apples = 450 This is the reason for technically calling gold as 'hedge against inflation'. That means, Gold always keeps pace with inflation and is not a wealth creation tool. At least, it is said so in the present times. Advisers in India expect an average return of 5% to 7% per annum from gold in the long term, at par with inflation rate.

Gold is an asset. Gold means wealth. But in India, it is a lot more than that. Gold is a part of life. It is a way of life. I know you agree with me because, a man's (of course woman is too) relationship with gold begins when he is born into this world and will only end when he leaves this world. It is one metal (and one thing) that Indians are attached to irrespective of age, region, and religion than anything else. You may want to double the gold worn on you but never think of cutting it down even if it is a little uncomfortable. Have you ever heard a dame say, I do not want a gold ring, or a chain or a necklace? Indians rarely buy gold with the idea of selling for a profit. They may pawn or loan gold ornaments to meet financial needs but never sell or part with them. Had you bought 1 ounce of gold (31.1034 grams) on 01-Jan-1980 for 4190/- (135/- per gram), it would be worth 89900/- today. Do you know what that means in terms of annualised rate of return? That is a return of 9.40%. At least if you had bought gold when the price went down two years later to 2900, your compounded annual growth rate would be 11.30% p.a. If you had bought it another two years later for 3900, your return would be 11%. But, if you say these are all old stories, let us look at the new ones. Had you bought 1-ounce gold ten years back for 17200, the returns calculate to 18% per annum. If you say you already know how gold created wealth over the centuries, the question is, have you bought gold for investment and not for ornamental purpose?

The two illustrations above may seem contradictory. In one paragraph I said gold acts as a hedge against inflation and the next I showed how gold created wealth in the long term. The idea is to tell you how gold may create wealth in the exceedingly long term while in the short term it can be volatile like equity and is influenced by may factors some of which may not be foreseeable except for believing in sentiments and trends that may or may not repeat. A report by the US Geological Society mentioned that the gold reserves in 2012 were 51000 tonnes globally. This is after mining 2560 tonnes in 2010 and another 2700 tonnes in the year 2011. With that kind of increase in production year-on-year, the gold reserves were estimated to last for another 13 years. That means gold mines across the globe will be completely depleted by the year 2025. But that is only the supply side of the story. With countries like China producing an average of 350 tonnes of gold every year that does not leave the country, comparatively very low reserves with our central bank, an estimated 18000 tonnes of gold stacked in the hands of the people of India in the form of jewellery and an average of 1.5 Crore weddings per year estimated for the next ten years in India alone, the ever increasing demand for gold among the public and the governments alike is surely going to take gold prices through the roof like never before. With a majority of Chinese buying high quality 24 Karat gold, 1. 30 billion Indians securing their jewellery in lockers forever and 350 million Americans (third largest nation in terms of population) finding new fashion trends with gold, where do you think the gold prices will be when there are no mines to dig out gold? (References are taken from the website of the World Gold Council.) Another interesting story I encountered on the internet some time back was that reported by multiple sources that did rounds for some time was that a good number of states in the US are seeking permission to introduce and use gold and silver currency as they lost confidence in their federal reserve and are in the final stages of the process. Tells a story, does it not? A wise reader can certainly visualize how, over the next two to three decades, micro changes that are happening now, can aggregate to bring macroeconomic changes in India and the world-over. If you still think that the story of gold is over, it is okay. You know what you know.

Now, if you have decided to go ahead and invest in gold, particularly at every dip, then the next question is, what form should you buy it in? What is the convenient way of buying gold? You know you cannot buy 1-gram gold coin from the bank. And, for some of us, 5 grams may be too much to invest on a monthly or regular basis. Moreover, you may laugh it off or ridicule it, but the risk of losing it to the robbers is always present. The risk only goes down but not eliminated when you store it in a locker with the bank, thereby increasing the costs. If you are still okay with all that and want to buy gold in physical form, that is all right. You can start a monthly investment scheme with a gold shop or buy randomly from banks or showrooms on auspicious days or whenever you want to. However, in today's developed world, it is recommended that you buy goal in securitised form i.e. either in the form of gold exchange traded funds or through gold fund of funds, which in turn invest in the gold exchange traded funds. Gold ETFs track the price of physical gold, which is held by the issuing fund house. Since the fund houses have gold deposits against the units they issue to the buyers, value of one unit of gold corresponds one gram of physical gold. This supplies an opportunity to invest in gold from the comfort of one's home. Furthermore, there is no risk of theft and increased costs in the form of locker etc. A lay-customer may be confused when he sees a different unit price for each fund house that is offering the ETFs. However, be advised that the unit price is irrelevant in the case of gold ETFs and the difference between the net asset values of various schemes is due to a range of factors. As the units are traded on the stock exchanges by investors at large, sometimes a buyer is willing to pay extra to buy a unit while a seller, sometimes is ready to compromise on the price if he needs money. Another reason is the charges or what it is technically called - the expense ratio. I am not saying that the expense ratio vastly differs. Suppose X fund charges 1.45%, Y fund charges 1.50%. The difference is only 0.05% i.e. on a unit value of say 3000, the difference amounts to Rs. 1.50. But, be advised that the NAV or unit price you see on the exchanges is net of the expense ratio. So, when you calculate your returns, you do not have to discount the charges from the profits. Exchange-traded funds may not always invest 100% of the monies in gold. A small portion may be usually invested in debt & money market products and some is maintained as cash reserve. Also, the root-mean-square of the difference between the gold ETF and the spot gold (also called as tracking error) ranges from usually 0.05% to 0.07%. All these reasons add up to the difference among the unit prices of schemes managed by various fund houses. There is no problem of liquidity either, as these are listed on the bourses. As to the taxation, since this is categorized as a mutual fund, investment in gold exchange traded funds is exempt from wealth tax and securities transaction tax. However, the sale proceeds are subject to long term and short-term capital gains tax as applicable. The only difference between the ETF and the Fund of Fund is that, in case of the latter, you can start a systematic investment plan or the SIP directly with the AMC. In case you want to sell, the AMC will buy the units directly from you, without you having to find a buyer on the exchange (not that you will not usually find buyers on the exchange). Alternatively, you cannot start a SIP in case of an ETF. However, some big brokers lately have started providing this tailor-made facility to their customers. So, check out with your broker if you are interested only in ETF and not the FOF.

Realty

Real Estate has been the cherry pick of Indians for ages. But the trend turned into obsession in the last half century. The youth, in present days, no sooner are they through with their higher education and landing up in some job, go for a housing loan and buy property. This happens either because they are too excited seeing ample money in their hands and want to accumulate wealth for themselves. Sometimes, they want to appease their parents too. What everyone fails to notice is that they are not just acquiring property, but they are creating a huge liability that they will carry until their middle age, for 20 years or so. And, (this is important) those who encourage them to buy property do not journey with them through the years and render proper advice when the latter is striving to pay off the liability and suffering from compromised cashflows. Property bought through loan, though convenient enough, usually eats away lion's share of an individual's savings potential often leaving one with meagre or no cash at all. Since the property bought will not be used to sell off and create pension or regular income in old age, and the future growth in earnings is used to adjust towards the increasing prices and changing lifestyle and planning for other needs and goals, critical needs are usually left out, unplanned. Alternately, individuals may consider buying a piece of land in the suburban, if they can identify a scheme that allows payment in instalments. However, appreciation of such an investment takes many years and even after exhibiting such remarkable patience, non-development in the geography where the property is located will prove disheartening.

Among similar others, real estate or property is one asset class that needs huge capital to invest in, except when someone is borrowing but it rewards the investors handsomely in the long-term. However, there are drawbacks. Liquidity is the first hurdle in property. Suppose one has dire need for money and gets ready to sell the property, but the market is so low, and prices have drastically come down that even if the person is ready to part with it at a reduced price, finding a buyer may not be so easy. Added to that, political uncertainty, and high expenses for either of the party might prevent one from being able to sell the asset.

Asset allocation

There are several types of asset allocation strategies that evolved over a period. Selection of the strategy depends on one's individual preference, knowledge one possess, time one can spend, and tools one can buy that are necessary for continuous monitoring. From among the many strategies that are in practice, we shall discuss now three viz. Strategic Asset Allocation, Tactical Asset Allocation and Dynamic Asset Allocation.

Strategic asset allocation: This is what we just saw at the beginning of the page. You create an asset mix like I showed above and no matter what, you stick to the asset classes. That means, whether the investment value goes up or down, you do not disturb the investments and hold on to them. It is nothing but the well-known 'buy & hold' strategy. One does not need to spend time analysing and evaluating the investments, following the trends in the economy and markets etc. Alternatively, those who are not keen about adopting this method can choose to rebalance the asset mix occasionally. There is no definite period as to how often one should rebalance the portfolio. Rebalancing means that if for several reasons, say equity has gone up and the debt portfolio is down, book profit in equity and invest more money in debt thereby bringing the asset allocation back to its original level.

Tactical asset allocation: Say, you are following strategic asset allocation. You have a gut feeling (do not depend on it though) or you observed that a sector and strong companies within that sector can benefit in the short term. Or, you expect that the quarterly financial results of a company are going to be attractive and see an opportunity to make a bit of extra return in the short term. Contrary to the Strategic asset allocation you have been following, you squeeze money from various sources including other asset classes and invest in the opportunity. When you achieved your objective of benefiting from the short-term opportunity, you return to the original strategic asset allocation method. The objective of Tactical asset allocation is not to let go off any opportunity by tightly sticking to buy & hold strategy.

Dynamic asset allocation: You expect the equity markets to be bearish in the near future. To prevent losses in equity portfolio or to cut down the losses, you bring down the allocation to equity. And, when you think there's trend reversal in the market, you invest more in equity. The difference between rebalancing we talked about in Strategic asset allocation and what we do in Dynamic asset allocation is that, in strategic asset allocation, when say, equity is going down (to maintain equilibrium), we invest more in equity and sell when it is going up. In dynamic asset allocation, we do quite the opposite. We sell when equity is going down and buy when it is going up. Note that the above explanation is meaningful only in case of equity. That means you sell equity when the market is declining. However, in debt, you buy when the interest rates are going down. This is because you want to lock your investments at high rates for long term.

For most passive investors who cannot spare time to go through the management of asset mix, Strategic Asset Allocation is a convenient and suitable option. A periodic review on one's own or consultation with a professional for second opinion is recommended to ensure that the portfolio is progressing in line with the assigned needs and goals.

Realising financial goals

After budgeting, addressing critical needs, discovering investment risk profile, and deciding a suitable asset allocation strategy, financial goals must be prioritised and quantified. The net surplus cashflow must then be apportioned to various financial goals. In this section, we shall first understand how goals must be planned for and what kind of critical thinking is required for achieving without jeopardising them. We shall also look at various investment products that can help in achieving the goals. Each product is different in its own way and suits a specific set of goals. Choosing the right product for the goal is important while implementing the plan. These are explained in length below.

Goal Planning

You now know that Asset Allocation is critical to goal planning, and Risk Profiling to asset allocation. Assuming risk profile turned out to be aggressive and the corresponding asset allocation strategy suggested 80% in equity, 15% in debt and 5% in gold let us take the example of children higher education goal and build our understanding on it. An individual has a daughter aged five. The parents wish her to study engineering. They estimated the present cost of the study at Rs. 5 Lakhs and another Rs. 10 Lakhs for post-graduation. Considering the present age, the money will be required twelve years hence and for higher education, there is a time of sixteen years. Here, one should remember that the rate of inflation is different for various products and services. While food inflation and household expenses increase at a certain rate, expenses in the education industry, healthcare, tourism, entertainment etc. increase at different rates depending on a variety of factors. Supposing inflation in education is higher, at 10% per annum, the cost of Rs. 5 Lakhs will inflate to Rs. 15.70 Lakhs and the higher education expenditure of Rs. 10 Lakhs will inflate to Rs. 46 Lakhs in sixteen years.

Going by the asset allocation recommended by the risk profiling questionnaire, a monthly investment of Rs. 5200 must be invested towards college/graduation. Towards higher education due in sixteen years, a monthly investment of

Rs. 8700 must be invested. These amounts can be invested separately with each amount in three asset classes in which case, 5% on 5200 in gold comes to an odd figure of Rs. 260. So, where will you invest Rs. 260 in gold monthly? It is almost impractical. Investing 5% separately again on 8700 comes to Rs 435. Alternately, you may club both and divide Rs. 14000 per month (rounded-off) as 11200 into equity, 2100 into debt and 700 into gold. When the first milestone is reached after twelve years, only the investment of Rs. 8700 will continue as 7000, 1300 and 400 in the three asset classes respectively for four more years. Alternately, an experienced financial planner tells you to invest single amount of Rs. 14750 per month for collective term of sixteen years for two goals, instead of adding two separate amounts of 5200 and 8700 for two different periods and dropping one midway, when a goal is achieved. You may divide the single amount of Rs. 14750 among the three asset classes as 11800 in equity, 2200 in debt and 750 in gold.

Is not financial planning about protecting one's monetary interests by taking cover from uncertainty to the best possible extent? Imagine a scenario in which two years before the goal year, a trend reversal begins in the markets and by the time funds are required, the goal corpus is down by 15%. During such a period, would you continue to stay invested in the same asset allocation for 11.1% average return or if recommended, you will shift to a conservative portfolio, preserve the accumulated wealth, and be satisfied with a return of +8% than see -15%? I am not literally asking what you would prefer but saying that the latter is better. A year or two before the goal year, it is sensible to protect the accumulated corpus by switching it to Debt (provided, Debt is favourable then) in addition to diverting the upcoming monthly investments until the goal is achieved. However, such an action is advocated subject to the then prevailing fundamentals and trends.

Goal protection

If you remember, while calculating life insurance requirement, we included responsibilities such as children higher education also. Few years ago, as the investment world was advancing, critical thinkers and analysts produced an idea to protect investors' financial goals, such as education. This is the idea. Why are we adding the cost of the need to life insurance requirement? Because, when the bread-earner is not around, the family is financially compensated to meet their needs, right? Had the earning member survived, he or she would have made regular investments as necessary (suggested by the financial plan) until the goal is achieved, would not you agree? So, what is more important here? Is it receiving of a hefty sum of money towards a goal that is due many years away or to ensure that the proposed investments continue as initially planned, until the goal year? While both help in protecting the need, the latter suffices the requirement with less financial burden. Let me explain. Recollect the future cost of the higher education goal and the related life insurance cover we considered in the HLV section of the previous chapter. The future cost of the need will be Rs. 2 Crores, which in present terms comes to Rs. 38 Lakhs. That aside, if the investments made towards the goal yield 12% rate of return, a monthly investment of Rs.42000 will have to be made. Now, the goal can be protected either by ensuring delivery of Rs. 38 Lakhs to the family or continuity of monthly investments of Rs. 42000 planned to be made until the goal year. In the case of the former, the individual will have extra cash outflow towards insurance premium on 38 Lakhs. However, mutual funds produced the idea that in the absence of the bread-earner, if the proposed monthly investments continue, the goal can be achieved equally. So, they integrated insurance with mutual funds so that the future instalments of SIP proposed by the deceased individual continue until the goal year, without any additional burden on him or the family, thereby fulfilling the need as planned. There are certain drawbacks though, to this arrangement. The amount of monthly investment that is eligible for insurance cover, the maximum amount of life insurance cover and the age of the individual proposing the SIP investment are restricted to certain limits. One must make study enough before depending on such arrangement and ensure that the scheme fits into the overall financial plan well.

Product Selection

Financial product selection is a complicated affair. Success of the entire, meticulously drafted plan depends on the selection of apt financial products. Before making an investment, one must study its features and check if the product meets the goal requirements. For example, the product must be liquid i.e. one must be able to sell or redeem or close the investment without any significant loss when the money is needed. If the investment has a specific maturity, one must make sure that such maturity occurs before the goal year or at least in the goal year. Investing in a product that is locked for ten years while the goal to which the investment is allocated is due in eight years is bad. In such a scenario, one is forced to borrow money for proportionately higher interest rate by pledging the apportioned investment or else some other liquid investment attached to another need or goal will have to be broken to accommodate the goal that is due immediately. Also, when a need or goal is sufficiently farther, one should be ready to invest in a risky product for not only a higher return but also to have some soothing on the present and near-future cash flows so that other financial needs or goals can be accommodated too, without extra financial burden. Similarly, if the goals are not far, one must not dare much and invest in risky or for that matter, even moderately risky products. Even if the return is lesser, given the limited time horizon for a specific goal, investing in a minimal risk product significantly protects the goal. If there will be a shortfall by investing in low-risk and low-return product, by tweaking the cashflows and allocation to other goals, contributions to the near and immediate goals may be increased. Such critical thinking is required to choose right financial products. I wish the reader will be careful with product-selection if planning on own or ask right questions if seeking help of an adviser. I believe advisers will know how well to do hence.

Notable Products

A product distributor might have a pounding heart while closing a deal with his client and jumping in joy, but an individual must never act in a hurry, while buying a product. Choosing a financial product to achieve a goal is a crucial part of financial planning process. We do not directly associate a product to a goal but divide them into distinct categories and understand them individually. That is because, sometimes a specific product type can be used to address more than one financial goal that have varying time horizons, while a product designed to address single financial goal may not be suitable in one's case due to differences in maturity period or return. The financial product universe is like a vast sea. Too many product categories, each containing so many products make it complicated to discuss everything. Hence, we shall review some important products for your general understanding. Certain long-term schemes that require minimum yearly payments are deactivated in case of default but require some penalty to be paid for reactivation. Some schemes also allow investments in the name of minors. Being a financial planner, I have missed such features that relate to situations I feel should not arise in the first place or to not encourage the reader to act in a certain way. One may refer respective product documentation for such details if they feel the urge or the need.

Small Savings Schemes

<u>National Savings Certificate</u>: It is the VIII Issue that is currently being offered. This certificate has a maturity of five years. It can be transferred only once to another person during the five-year period till maturity. Premature redemption of the certificate is not allowed. Minimum investment in the certificate is Rs. 100 and multiples thereof, without any maximum limit. With effect from January 01, 2019, the interest rate is 8% per annum compounded annually. The central government can increase or decrease the interest rate in any fiscal year. However, once an investor buys a certificate, the interest rate for that certificate continues for the entire term of five years. Investment in this certificate qualifies for tax benefit under Section 80C of the Income Tax Act. Though interest on the certificate is taxable on a yearly basis, it is assumed that the interest earned, because of the

annual compounding effect, is reinvested in the certificate, which is eligible for deduction. Hence, only in the year of maturity i.e. at the end of five years, as the last year's interest does not get reinvested, only that interest amount is taxable. Let us see one more example. Say you bought a certificate for Rs. 5000. At the end of five years, the maturity value of the investment will be Rs. 7346.64, including the interest of the last year that does not get reinvested. This interest is taxable as per the income tax slab that the tax assessee falls into. If the holder of the certificate is in say, 20% tax slab, 20% of the interest of Rs. 544.20, which is Rs. 108.84 is payable as tax. Thus, if the maturity value of Rs. 7346.64 is reduced by 108.84 to Rs. 7237.80, the effective return calculates to 7.68%. This is only an illustration. For someone who is in 10% tax slab or even higher or below the basic tax exemption limit specified under the Income Tax Act, the return calculation can be different. Non-resident Indians are not allowed to invest in this certificate.

<u>Monthly Income Scheme</u>: This product is designed to provide monthly cashflows to the investors. Contrary to the long-term nature of regular annuity or pension schemes, this has a maturity period of five years. Investment is allowed in multiples of Rs. 1500, with maximum limit of Rs. 4.50 Lakhs in case of single account and Rs. 9.00 Lakhs in case of joint account. With effect from January 01, 2019, the interest rate is 7.30% per annum payable monthly. The scheme can be prematurely closed after the first year but before completion of three years with a penalty of 2% discount on the deposit amount. Premature closure after third year attracts 1% discount on the deposit. Interest income received from this scheme is taxable as per the individual's income tax slab rate. Interest is credited to the savings account opened

at the post office where the investment was made or to the savings account opened at the CBS post offices.

<u>Senior Citizen Savings Scheme</u>: This scheme is comparable to the monthly income scheme but has higher interest rate and quarterly payment frequency. Individuals who are at least sixty years old are eligible to invest up to Rs. 15 Lakhs, in multiples of Rs. 1000. With effect from January 01, 2019, the interest rate is 8.70% per annum payable quarterly on 1st working day of April, July, October, and January each year until maturity. The scheme has a maturity period of five years but before expiry, it can be extended for a further period of three years. There is a penalty of 1.00% on the deposit if the account is closed after two years and 1.50% on the deposit, if the account is prematurely closed after the first year. However, closing the account during the extended period of three years does not attract any penalty. If the interest income in a fiscal year exceeds Rs. 10000, tax is deducted at source at 10% on the interest. Investment in this scheme qualifies for tax benefit under Section 80C of the Income Tax Act. Interest is credited to the savings account opened at the post office where the investment was made or to the savings account opened at the CBS post offices. On an investment of Rs. 15 Lakhs, the quarterly interest of Rs. 32625 at 2.18% per quarter aggregates to Rs. 1.30 Lakh per annum. In the absence of any other income, as per the prevailing income tax rules, the entire interest falls below the basic tax exemption limit and the tax liability of the senior citizen will be zero. Hence, the account holder may apply to the post office in writing to not deduct tax at source.

Public Provident Fund: This is hailed as one of the best social security schemes in India. The scheme has a maturity period of fifteen years from the end of the fiscal year in which the account is opened and often mistaken as fifteen years. If the investment is made at the beginning of the fiscal year i.e. first day of April, the investment matures at the end of the sixteenth year. One can apply for extension of the scheme in blocks of five years after maturity. Minimum investible amount in the scheme is Rs. 500 and the maximum limit is Rs. 1.50 Lakh. With effect from January 01, 2019, the interest rate is 8.00% per annum compounded yearly. However, the meaning of compounding in this case is different. Interest is calculated every month on the balance standing in the account on the fifth day. If the investment is made after fifth, interest is not calculated for that month. Interest amounts are thus calculated but credited to the provident fund account only at the end of the fiscal year. Its triple 'E' feature popularly called 'exempt-exempt-exempt' makes it a great investment for long-term goals such as retirement. Suppose you invest Rs. 1.50 Lakh on the first of every April until the last year. Your total investment of Rs. 22.50 Lakhs will grow to Rs. 44 Lakhs. Investment in this scheme qualifies for tax benefit under Section 80C of the Income Tax Act. Even the interest and maturity value are fully exempt from tax. There have been speculations in the industry for a long time that this feature can be removed by the government any time but fortunately, it has not happened yet. On the liquidity front, unlike other schemes we have seen so far, this account cannot be prematurely closed except during the extended blocks of five years after the completion of the original fifteen-year period. However, from the third fiscal year to the end of the sixth fiscal year, the scheme provides loan facility. The maximum amount of loan one can avail is limited to twenty-five percent of the balance standing in the account at the end of second fiscal years immediately preceding the year in which one applies for a loan. Interest on loan is charged at 2% higher than the prevailing interest rate on deposits for the quarter. Loan must be repaid within thirty-six months from the date the loan was disbursed. You do not want to know the repercussions if you do not clear the loan within the given period. From the seventh fiscal year, liquidity comes in the form of withdrawal facility. The amount allowed for withdrawal is either fifty percent of the balance standing in the account at the end of the immediately-preceding fourth year or the balance in the account at the end of the preceding year, whichever is lower. If you have your eyes set on the withdrawal and loan facilities, I request you to not invest in this scheme and destroy its purpose. Non-resident Indians are not allowed to invest in this scheme.

<u>Sukanya Samriddhi Yojana</u>: Regarded as an imitation of the public provident fund specially designed for the benefit of the girl child, certain benefits of this scheme supersede that of the former. Either parent or the legal guardian can open an account in the name of the girl child before she attains the age of ten. The account matures when the girl turns twenty-one. With effect from July 05, 2018, the minimum investible amount in the scheme is Rs. 250 and the maximum limit is Rs. 1.50 Lakh. With effect from January 01, 2019, the interest rate is 8.50% per annum compounded yearly. After the girl turns eighteen, a maximum withdrawal of fifty percent on the balance at the end of the immediately-preceding fiscal year can made. This scheme enjoys similar tax benefits as the public provident fund. Non-resident Indians are not allowed to invest in this scheme.

National Pension System

How it parallelly made public provident fund available to the citizens of the country similar to that of the employee's provident fund meant for those in service, the central government of India opened the subscription to the national pension system for all its citizens from May 01, 2009. The scheme is regulated by the Pension Fund Regulatory and Development Authority (PFRDA). Unlike the public provident fund, this scheme does not offer guaranteed, tax-free, and risk-free returns. In investment jargon, this can be compared to a balanced fund but with certain conditions. NPS is a defined-contribution plan in that a minimum amount must be invested every year failing which, the account will be frozen and can only be reactivate on payment of the penalty. Though returns are not guaranteed, professional management, asset allocation, diversification and particularly exceptionally low costs compared to any other investment makes it attractive enough to include in your basket of investments that are apportioned to retirement goal. Any citizen of India aged eighteen to sixty-five can subscribe to this scheme. Though non-resident Indians can contribute to this scheme subject to the foreign exchange and other regulations stipulated by the Reserve Bank, overseas citizens of India, persons of Indian origin and Hindu undivided families cannot open an NPS account.

The scheme offers two types of accounts viz. Tier I and Tier II. While Tier II account is liquid, meaning that monies can be withdrawn when needed, Tier I account is locked and is not accessible for withdrawals till maturity. Tier I account can be opened with Rs. 500. All subsequent transactions also must be a minimum of Rs. 500. However, the minimum yearly contribution to Tier I account is Rs. 1000. Tier II account can be opened with a minimum of Rs. 1000. All subsequent contributions must be a minimum of Rs. 250. There are no minimum and maximum contribution limits in the case of Tier II account. Investment choices available under the scheme are explained by PFRDA as follows.

Under NPS, how the money is invested will depend upon subscriber's own choice. NPS offers a number of funds and multiple investment options to choose from. In case the subscriber does not want to exercise a choice, the money will be invested as per the Default choice of "Moderate Life Cycle Fund" under "Auto Choice" option, where money will get invested in various type of schemes as per subscriber's age. The NPS offers two approaches to invest subscriber's money: In Active Choice, the subscriber will have the option to actively decide as to how the NPS pension wealth is to be invested in the following options:

- *Asset Class E: Investments in predominantly equity market instruments*
- *Asset Class C: Investments in fixed income instruments other than Government securities*
- *Asset Class G: Investments in Government securities*
- *Asset Class A: Investment in Alternative Investment Schemes*

Subscriber can choose to invest entire pension wealth in C or G asset classes and up to a maximum of 50% in equity (Asset class E) and up to a maximum of 5% in asset class "A". Subscriber can also distribute his/her pension wealth across E, C, G and A asset classes, subject to such conditions as may be prescribed by PFRDA.

NPS offers an easy option for those participants who do not have the required knowledge to manage their NPS investments. In case subscribers are unable/unwilling to exercise any choice as regards asset allocation, their funds will be invested in accordance with the Auto Choice option. In this option, the investments will be made in a life-cycle fund. Here, the proportion of funds invested across three asset classes will be determined by a pre-defined portfolio (which would change as per age of subscriber), with the investment in E decreasing and in C & G increasing with the age of the subscriber. Three Life Cycle funds are available under this Auto Choice:

(i) *LC75 – Aggressive Life Cycle Fund: In this Life Cycle Fund, the exposure in Equity Investments starts with 75% till age 35 and gradually reduces as per the age of the subscriber.*

(ii) *LC50- Moderate Life Cycle Fund: In this Life Cycle Fund, the exposure in Equity Investments starts with 50% till age 35 and gradually reduces as per the age of the subscriber.*

(iii) *LC 25- Conservative life cycle fund: In this Life Cycle Fund, the exposure in Equity Investments starts with 25% till age 35 and gradually reduces as per the age of the subscriber.*

The default auto choice if the subscriber is not choosing any of the above option is Moderate life Cycle Fund.

Upon attainment of the age of 60 years, at least 40% of the accumulated pension wealth of the subscriber needs to be utilized for purchase of annuity providing for monthly pension to the subscriber and balance is paid as lump sum payment to the subscriber. In case the total accumulated corpus is less than Rs. 2 Lacs, the subscriber may opt for 100% lumpsum withdrawal. However, the subscriber has the option to defer the lump sum withdrawal till the age of 70 years. Subscriber has also got the option to continue contributing up to the age of 70 years. This option is required to be exercised up to 15 days prior to completion of 60 years. At any time before attaining the age of 60 years, the subscriber may exit from NPS before attaining the age of 60 years, only if he has completed 10 years in NPS. At least 80% of the accumulated pension wealth of the subscriber needs to be utilized for purchase of annuity providing for monthly pension to the subscriber and the balance is paid as a lump sum payment to the subscriber. In case the total accumulated corpus is less than Rs. 1 Lac, the subscriber may opt for 100% lumpsum withdrawal. In such an unfortunate event of the death of the subscriber, option will be available to the nominee to receive 100% of the NPS pension wealth in lump sum. However, if the nominee wishes to continue with the NPS, he/she shall have to subscribe to NPS individually after following due 'Know Your Client' procedure.

At present, there are eight fund managers appointed by PFRDA to manage your monies under this scheme. These pension fund managers are –

- *Birla SunLife Pension Management Limited*
- *HDFC Pension Management Company Limited*
- *ICICI Prudential Pension funds Management Company Limited*
- *Kotak Mahindra Pension Fund Limited*
- *LIC Pension Fund Limited*
- *Reliance Capital Pension Fund Limited*
- *SBI Pension Funds Private Limited*
- *UTI Retirement Solutions Limited*

You can select any pension fund manager of your choice and change it once every year without any charge, if you want to. The fund managers manage your monies as per the guidelines issued and are overseen by the PFRDA.

Endowment Plans

Going by the fundamentals explained about insurance plans initially, you already know that if there is any savings element in a non-market linked insurance plan, it is an endowment plan by nature. These plans come in various names and types viz. Whole-life plan, Education endowment plan, Marriage endowment plan, Return of premium etc. However, one of the most popular products of all time in the Indian insurance sector, money back plans have been favoured by the urban and rural population for their seemingly attractive periodic cashbacks throughout the tenure. Though they fall under the endowment plans category, they are also identified as a category of their own. These policies have a tenure of twenty or twenty-five years and make cash payments at intervals of four or five years. These are participating policies but non-linked meaning, the policy holder is entitled for a share in the profits earned by the company under the policy, but the performance of the policy is not dependent on the markets. These policies usually have both guaranteed and variable returns. Let us take the example of a 35-year old individual, who buys a 25-year moneyback policy with a premium paying term of twenty years. For a sum assured or risk cover of Rs. 1 Lakh, he pays an annual premium of Rs. 6000. The policy offers moneyback of Rs. 15000 at the end of the fifth, tenth, fifteenth and twentieth years and at the end of twenty-five-year period, a final estimated payment of Rs. 1.25 Lakhs, all benefits included and adjustment of various expenses and mortality charges towards death benefit. Though the benefits are calculated at an estimated 8% per annum, the actual internal rate of return turns out to be between a meagre 4.30% and 4.40%. With high inflation rates killing the purchasing power of our hard-earned money constantly, one should reflect and decide whether the return on schemes that appear lucrative are worth investing or not. While the insurance policy enjoys tax benefit under Section 80C, the cash payments received from the policy as moneyback are treated as income and may attract income tax liability depending on the personal financial profile.

Chit-fund Schemes

Native to India, this scheme is known across the length and breadth of the country, regardless of literacy, education, and income levels, even more widespread than life insurance and moneyback plans. On encountering even slightest volatility in market-linked investments, people resort to chit funds, considering them better yielding and stable investments. It is hence necessary to understand them in comparison to other investment categories and when it comes to comparing investments, there is nothing more meaningful than the rate of return. Let us understand this concept through an illustration.

Imagine twenty people coming together and mutually agreeing to start a cooperative scheme. The scheme helps those who need money and rewards others with return on their investment. The scheme is run by one of the persons who is usually called a Foreman. Suppose the value of the chit is Rs. 2 Lakhs and the period is twenty months. Each person contributes Rs. 10000 per month. However, the members do not always pay the same amount. In a month, one of the subscribers needed money urgently. However, owing to his emergency, the member bid to take less than Rs. 2 Lakhs, which is the chit value say, Rs. 1.60 Lakh i.e. a discount of 20%. Out of this, the foreman may charge 5% of the chit value as his commission i.e. out of Rs. 40000, Rs. 10000 goes as the commission. The remaining amount of Rs. 30000 is divided by the number of members in the scheme, which comes to Rs. 1500 per member. This amount which the bidding member has foregone and distributed among the members, is called discount. Now, the members must pay only Rs. 8500 (=10000-1500). Thus, return in the case of chit fund comes in the form of discounted premiums and the chit value is returned to the members at the end of the term, whoever have not bid throughout the period of twenty months. If we calculate the percentage of the discount, it comes to 15% of the monthly subscription amount. Either out of ignorance or because of not paying special attention or out of necessity or any other reason, chit fund investors usually mistake this return to compounded annual growth rate, such as the bank fixed deposit rate, which compounds annually throughout the deposit period. However, the actual return from a chit fund is far less in comparison to other investments. Besides, one must remember that the risk of default or fraud in unorganised chit funds is exceedingly high and that kind of risk is incomparable to strategic and fundamentally sound investments such as equity, mutual funds, unit linked insurance plans and all other small savings schemes that we have discussed above.

Mutual Funds

Though I meant to discuss about mutual funds in a separate chapter considering its voluminous nature, to keep it simple and discuss the fundamental aspects of the product and some additional information, I am discussing it here. Treat this as a power-point presentation or a quick class for a common investor to get the gist of it rather than a technical, elaborate, and critical long-term course for a student of investments. One of the most suitable, flexible, and transparent products in the Indian investment universe, mutual fund is a great medium for achieving investment goals. While a large urban population is already acquainted with mutual funds, majority across the breadth of the country is yet uninformed or averse to it, either due to inhibition or a past adverse experience that was a result of uninformed decisions.

<u>Why mutual funds?</u> When you must invest for a goal, the question 'where to invest' arises. We have already seen what kinds of asset classes exist. Which one suits our needs? Researchers, analysts, and advisers throughout the world agree that in the long term, Equity is the best asset class among all that can fulfil financial goals. Equity in general sense refers to equity shares of companies, whether they are listed on stock exchanges or not, such as the Bombay Stock Exchange and the National Stock exchange. But how would you know which companies to invest in? You will have to do the following.

- Constantly follow the news and evaluate every bit of it. Study and understand which way the economy is heading. Though you cannot predict, you should know if the interest rate will go up or down.

Understand the economic policy of the RBI. Be able to estimate the influence of economic indicators like wholesale price index, consumer price index, index for industrial production, fiscal deficit etc. on the markets – both debt and equity.

- After churning all the global economic and political data, understand which sectors can benefit in the prevailing situations; evaluate the demand and supply condition presently and in the future for various goods and services; know the import and export situation for all these goods and services, identify the sectors that can benefit in the present tax, economic and political situations, if you want exposure to commodities too, follow the agrarian reforms, the monsoons, the announcements of meteorological department etc. Interested in metals? Study the reports of world gold council, commodity exchanges etc.
- Study the individual companies and investment products that are favourable under the above conditions. Invest in diverse types of products and continue to evaluate them by following up with the above research.
- Dynamically, rebalance your portfolio and asset classes and benefit from the short-term opportunities that arise in various markets related to the asset mix like steep price correction in gold, higher interest rates, great quarterly financial results etc. Book profit when the time is right. Combine all the above asset allocation strategies.

If you cannot do all the above yourself for reasons whatever, delegate the responsibility to a professional fund manager who shall take care of all the above for you, for a fee. That is what a mutual fund does! All you need to do is find a proven fund manager, believe in him, and let him do his job. Does not it sound like a great relief? You just must select a good fund that can help with your goals and leave it to the fund manager to meticulously drive the growth of your investment.

<u>Categorisation:</u> Based on which asset class they invest in, SEBI, vide Circular No. SEBI/HO/IMD/DF3/CIR/P/2017/114 dated October 06, 2017, classified mutual funds as Equity schemes, Debt schemes, Hybrid schemes, Solution oriented schemes, and Other schemes. Under these broader heads are categories of mutual funds that gives a better idea of the specific type of funds they are. The categories of equity funds specified by SEBI are Multi cap, Large cap, Mid cap, Small Cap, Dividend yield, Value, Contra, Focused, Sectoral or Thematic and ELSS.

CLASS	CATEGORY			
Equity Schemes	Multi Cap	Large Cap	Large & Mid Cap	MidCap
	Small cap	Dividend Yield	Value*	Contra*
	Focused	Sectoral / Thematic	ELSS	
	*Mutuals will be permitted to offer either Value or Contra.			
Debt Schemes	Overnight**	Liquid $**	Ultra Short Duration	Low Duration
	Money Market	Short Duration	Medium Duration	Medium to Long Duration
	Long Duration	Dynamic Bond	Corporate Bond	Credit Risk^
	Banking and PSU	Gilt	10-year Gilt	Floater
	** Uniform cut-off timings specified by SEBI for applicability of NAV must be followed			
	$ All provisions mentioned in SEBI circular SEBI/IMD/CIR No.13/150975/09 shall be applicable			
Hybrid Schemes	Conservative Hybrid	Balanced Hybrid @	Aggressive Hybrid @	Dynamic Asset Allocation
	Balanced Advantage	Multi Asset Allocation##	Arbitrage	Equity Savings
	@ Mutuals will be permitted to offer either an Aggressive Hybrid or Balanced			
	## Foreign securities will not be treated as a separate asset class			
Solution Oriented	Retirement	Children's		
Other Schemes	Index / ETFs	FoFs (Overseas / Domestic)		

Large cap funds invest in blue chip companies, which are industry leaders. The market capitalisation of these companies is large, and they have significant market share in the kind of products they sell e.g. companies in the Nifty 50 index or Sensex 30, top 100 companies by market capitalisation etc. In line with the definition of large cap stocks by SEBI, AMFI prepared a list of stocks that are considered large cap. These are top 100 companies by market capitalisation and their market cap ranged from Rs. 30000 Crores (approx. 4.28 Billion USD) and upwards. Such companies are well established with loyal customer base and greater geographical presence. Though their net profits go up or down quarter-on-quarter, usually we do not see them making losses, except in exceptional cases where suitable investment decisions are not taken. Their share prices are less volatile and correspondingly their growth is stable. Within the equity funds class, large cap is considered lower risk category, compared to others. Under a large cap scheme, at least 80% of the funds or assets it manages get invested in large cap companies. Large cap or blue-chip funds are more suitable for investors who are investing in equity for the first time and have a minimum period of three to five years, depending on the trend in the markets they are entering. Remember well that the longer the holding period of the investment, less significant the time of entry into the market is.

Mid cap funds invest in medium sized companies by market capitalisations. Going by the definition, market capitalisation of these companies ranges from Rs. 10000 Crores to Rs. 30000 Crores. In 2019, these are 150 in number. They may not be as large as blue-chip or large cap companies, but they are large enough with decent market share in their product and service segments and have the potential to grow to the size of a large one. Compared to large cap, they are riskier as they have tough competition from the larger companies and smaller ones. But commensurate with the risk, the growth of such companies and returns therefrom are usually greater than those of the large cap. Investors willing to bear risk for achieving medium to long term goals i.e. at least five years to seven years, may choose to invest in such schemes. Riskier Small cap funds are recommended for a minimum time horizon of ten years and above, but they yield better return than large and mid-cap categories. In case of mid and small cap schemes, at least 65% assets get invested in mid cap and small cap companies as defined by SEBI.

There are also combinations of various categories such as large and mid-cap, multi-cap etc. Depending on the proportion of allocation, risk on account of such categorisation varies. Sectoral or Thematic funds focus their investment in companies belonging to a single or few related sectors such as pharma, technology, banking, infrastructure etc. They are not comparable with other categories but riskier than diversified small cap funds. Such funds must invest at least 80% of the assets in specific sector or theme as declared in their scheme objective. Investing in schemes categorised as Equity Linked Savings Scheme (ELSS) offer tax deduction benefit and have a statutory lock-in period of three years.

<u>Scheme Selection</u>: Return is the key for any investment. Higher the return, the better. If not for return, why does any person put his money into a product or business? Hence, it is only natural that an investor, while choosing an investment (in this context, a mutual fund scheme), looks at returns of various schemes and whichever delivered highest return in the past and has the highest 'Star' rating given by an agency, puts the money into it. However, an adviser is not supposed or expected to do the same. Otherwise, there exists

no difference between a lay-investor and a professional. I do not say that star-rating methodology of the rating agencies is irrational, but I say that it must not be solely depended upon. An adviser is expected to make a value addition, not merely agree to the investor's selection. To select a scheme, an adviser must look beyond past returns. There are two types of information one should look at – the fundamental and technical characteristics. It begins with the selection of fund house or the Asset Management Company (AMC). Why does the fund house matter? Some look at goodwill while others look at the broader investment philosophy and principles. Many-a-time I heard people rejecting a fund house right on hearing the name. If we unite distinct reasons for rejecting the funds, will there be anything left for us to invest in this product category? When it comes to investments, we need to take out the emotions and judge the fund dispassionately. Once the fund houses are shortlisted, fund managers are selected based on factors such as their overall fund management experience, experience with the fund house and if the fund manager moved in from another company, how the schemes he managed earlier fared etc. An experienced fund manager may manage more than one or two schemes that are spread across various categories within the equity or debt asset classes. If one reads a mutual fund factsheet, the first thing they would see is a scheme's objective. At a bird's eye view, the objective broadly describes the scheme's strategy i.e. market capitalisation of companies, number of companies, objective to provide long-term return or income or both etc. With the passage of time and the regulator's new guidelines pertaining to categorisation of schemes, it has become easier understand the general nature of a scheme and the objective is hardly looked at, by anyone. Every now and then, an educated investor may doubt if the AUM (Assets Under Management) held under a single scheme has any impact on scheme's performance. Not always but depending on the size of the companies in which the scheme with large AUM invests, their liquidity, expenses incurred in managing the fund, calls of the fund manager to deploy fresh monies received into the scheme and redemption pressures etc. can influence the returns in either direction. Latest regulations mandate that the expense ratio in mutual funds be lower as the assets increase, which benefits investors but not favourable to distributors. Historical existence of the scheme i.e. number of years since inception, total number of scrips held under the scheme, concentration of the portfolio among top ten companies and top five sectors etc. tell whether a portfolio is well diversified or over-diversified or concentrated among companies. Usually, companies with no correlation between one another are preferred but the effect of such a measure may be limited. All these form part of the fundamental aspect of the scheme selection process. Once the investor is satisfied with these and narrowed down a list of schemes, further analysis is required in the form of technical aspects. Let us go through these one-by-ones.

Risk in investment parlance is of two types. While one type of risk involves erosion of the principal, i.e. reduction in the original amount you invested, the other risk involves earning a lesser return than required. We have already seen the jeopardy of the second type before. Technically, two words are used to refer to risk associated with an investment and they are 'Standard Deviation' and 'Beta'. Do not fret. I am not going deep into the calculation methodology for these technical parameters. All that you will see here is how to read and understand these figures if you ever see them. Standard deviation tells you how much the average return you expected can fluctuate. Suppose you narrowed down to two large cap mutual fund schemes. One has given a return of 14.95% and the other 15.05%. But the standard deviation of the former is 19 while the latter has 24. It is better to choose the one with 14.95% return because, comparatively the investment has lesser risk associated with it while the returns are closer and comparable to the other investment. One disadvantage of the standard deviation is that, it tells us how much our return can deviate from the expected return on the upside as well as the downside. For example, an investment is expected to give a return of 10% and the standard deviation is 5, it means your actual returns (not always but most of the time) fluctuate between 9.50% and 10.50% i.e. -0.50 and +0.50 of the 10% expected return. So, as a nonprofessional, when you are reading standard deviation, this is what you should think. Am I comfortable with -1%, -2%, -3%, -5%, -7%, -10% etc.? Now, if you have tolerance for deviation of 10% (with the hope that your return can also be higher than expected) and the expected return on the investment you chose is 15%, your actual return can be anywhere between 13.50% & 16.50%. This does not cancel out the possibility of lesser return than 13.50% or higher return than 16.50%. It only means that most of the time the actual return falls in this range. I hope you understood now, what the term means or how to understand it when you see the figure. Remember that standard deviation is also called unsystematic risk or diversifiable risk. That means, by diversifying the investment well among many companies belonging to various sectors, the risk associated can be minimised (not eliminated). The only important thing is not to over-diversify. As we already know 'higher the risk, higher the return', because of over-diversification, both, the risk, and return go down. So, one should have a well-diversified portfolio but not over-diversified or under-diversified. So, if standard deviation is low, should you go ahead and buy the product? No. You need more information.

Then next thing you should understand is the 'Beta'. Beta is also called Systematic Risk or Market Risk. Unlike standard deviation, this cannot be diversified away which means, this market risk cannot be minimized by diversifying the portfolio as in the case of standard deviation. If the beta figure is 1 (can be read as 100%), it means that the volatility of the investment is at par with the market (or benchmark) i.e. if the market goes up by 5%, our investment goes up by 5% and if the market is down by 3%, our investment too goes down by 3% and so on. If beta is greater than 1, it implies that our investment is less volatile than the market. Market in this context is to be read as 'index' or 'benchmark'. If say beta is 1.15, and the market appreciates by 10%, our investment or portfolio goes up by 11.5% (higher volatility than the index). It also means that if market falls by 10%, our investment value depreciates by 11.5%. On the other hand, if beta is 0.9 and the benchmark rises by 10%, your investment will yield only 9%. If the index dives by 10%, you will lose only 9%. This shows that low beta means lesser volatility than the market. Again, it also means lesser return than the market. Particularly, beta is widely and importantly used in evaluating mutual funds. That explains why you see this figure in the fund factsheets of mutual funds, without a miss.

I can say that after reading the next few lines, your perception, and ways of choosing an investment – particularly, an equity-oriented mutual fund or any other similar investment will change, forever. But it will be best if I illustrate this through an example, which goes thus. A college confers an award to the best student at the end of the last term, which is after four years of course study. For simplicity, let us say there are five students (and not fifty – too complicated). This is how the students scored in each of the years.

Student	Year 1	Year 2	Year 3	Year 4	Average	Std. Dev.	Sharpe
A	40	55	50	65	52.5	10.41	0.72
B	50	40	55	50	48.75	6.29	0.6
C	65	35	40	70	52.5	17.56	0.43
D	35	45	45	55	45	8.16	0
E	55	50	50	55	52.5	2.89	2.6

Once you understand the figures above, you will know that they tell you quite a story. Five students, A, B, C, D and E have earned scores as shown in the above table during the four years of their study in the college. You can see the average of their scores over the four-year period. And, you already know the standard deviation (the column next to average), which is calculated based on the consistency of the marks they scored. The standard deviation shows how risky their performance and methods of study is. You can see that students A, C & E have the same average of 52.50. But, whom do you award the trophy? To decide, we need to do two things. First, see how consistent they are year-on-year. Second, compare the average with the benchmark performance. Here, the lowest average any student is 45.00. So, you know that anything above 45 is a superior performance and choose this as a base score or benchmark for comparison. Student A has standard deviation of 10.41 based on his consistency, student C has 17.56 and student E has a risk of 2.89. Now, comparing the average and standard deviation with the benchmark score of 45, we get the ratios shown in the last column to the right and this is what is called the 'Sharpe' ratio. A, with the same average as C and E, has a Sharpe ratio of 0.72; and C, with the same average, has Sharpe ratio of 0.43. On the other hand, E has a Sharpe ratio of 2.60 though his average is same as that of A & C. What does it tell us? Sharpe ratio is high when the risk is low, and returns are high, which in the illustration above means low standard deviation and good average score. Do not you think E qualifies for the award? Of course, you do. If you understood the practical implication of the Sharpe ratio, start using it when selecting an investment. The best thing here is that you do not need to calculate this ratio yourself. It is hell of a job to work on the stuff. You see the figure pertaining to an investment and you know that 'bigger, the better'.

Moving forward, how do you rate a fund manager (heavy stuff do not you say)? How do you know that so-and-so fund manager is a better one than his peers? It is simple. While comparing similar investments, the one who delivered highest return is the best, right? Technically, we do the same thing but instead of the peers, here we compare the returns delivered by the fund manager with that of a benchmark. What I am talking about is, 'Alpha'. For example, if Alpha is 3, it means that the fund manager delivered 3% better return than that of the benchmark. Or, if the alpha is -5, then the fund manager gave -5% than the benchmark return. Convenient is it not? So, higher Alpha means, better fund management.

Before we conclude this section, there is just one more thing – comparing an investment with the peer group to settle with the best. So, how to do it? Do you say, 'this melon is sweeter than the lemon' or 'this melon is sweeter than the one I had before'? Which statement sounds right? The latter, is it not? What do you understand from that? - that you should compare apples with apples and oranges with oranges. Also, if you say, 'this apple is good', it gives a message but, if you can tell how good the apple is, do not you think the message will be clear enough? But, how can you tell how good the apple is? By comparing it with another one of course! This 'another one' in mutual fund parlance is called the 'Benchmark' whose sole purpose is, to be compared with a scheme. If I say that my portfolio performed better than the benchmark, it sends a message. But, let me say, your portfolio of investment has 25 large cap stocks and the benchmark with which you are comparing has a portfolio of 80 stocks distributed among large and mid-cap stocks. Am I right in comparing the two? For example, the fund objective of a scheme says, 'to invest in 30 large cap companies from among the top 200 by market capitalization' (or total value of the company, for simplicity). Simplifying it further, it means that any point of time, the scheme stays invested in 30 companies only. The scheme chooses an index that has 200 companies in it. Is there a relation? 30 compared with 200? How meaningful is it? This comparison is technically called 'Correlation' or 'R-squared' also written as 'R^2'. The higher the correlation with the benchmark, more meaningful Beta and Alpha of the scheme are. However, one must remember that the scheme does not replicate the index in which case, it becomes a passively managed index fund and the rules of scheme-selection may change altogether.

You have understood so far, some of the most important technical terms that are profoundly important in selecting an equity-oriented basket product in the likes of a mutual fund. But, going back to the original question, how do you select an investment? Based on the 'Standard Deviation, or looking at the 'Beta', or the high 'Alpha' or a great 'Sharpe' ratio? Let us say, you are impressed by the Alpha of a fund and decided to invest in it. Let me ask you, 'doesn't it matter to you how the fund manager of the scheme where you invested, was able to deliver better returns (or better alpha), while other fund managers in the same category of investments could not?' Suppose you invested in a flexi-cap fund thinking that majority of the assets is in large cap companies. However, six months later, the fund manager changed the strategy (though within the purview of the objective), and shifted the allocation to mid-cap and small cap. Let us take another scenario. A scheme usually invests in many companies, say 100, which you can almost call 'over-diversified'. And, that is the kind of investment you have been looking for. However, a year later, you revisited the portfolio and saw that there are only 45 companies in the scheme. That may be the ideal number to have but you neither anticipated nor comfortable with that. The strategic changes that we discussed resulted in better rate of return than the peer group. Does 'Alpha' alone mean a lot to you without studying other fundamental facts? Let us suppose that the fundamentals behind alpha are good. What about correlation? Instead of the ideal 90%, it is just 65%. Are you happy about it just because the alpha is great? What I am saying is, all these parameters must be read and understood in relation to one another but not independently. Some equally important ratios that seem more logical and appealing such as the Sortino Ratio and Information Ratio are appearing in mutual fund factsheets for some time now. One should understand these too and consider them fund selection.

<u>Investment process</u>: When it finally comes to making actual investment, two questions arise – 'should I make a one-time investment, or can I invest periodically also?' 'what is the minimum stipulated amount for investing in mutual funds?'. Well, you can do both in mutual funds. Whichever scheme you invest in, when you invest in the schemes of a

mutual fund for the first time, similar to a bank account number, a Folio Number is allotted. The folio number stands as a reference number to record and track all buy and sell transactions made through that folio. The next time you invest in schemes of the same mutual fund, if you give the reference of the folio number, new purchase will be added to the existing folio number. But if you do not, a new folio number is created, and mutual fund Units are allotted to the new folio, which means you will have to keep a record of two folios or account numbers. Of course, you can merge them into one later, if you wish. When you buy or invest in companies, you are allotted equity shares. Likewise, in mutual funds, you are allotted Units. However, you can buy shares only in multiples of one while in case of mutual funds, you are allotted units up to one-thousandth of a unit also, which means, you can buy units for a standard amount (rounded-off) instead of buying units and paying to the last paisa. For example, if you invest Rs. 10000 and the cost of one unit is Rs. 13, you get allotted 769.231 units. You do not have to pay Rs. 9997 to get rounded off units of 769 precisely.

Investment can be a Lump sum (one-time) purchase or periodic. Application made to a mutual fund to invest at monthly or quarterly frequency is called Systematic Investment Plan (SIP). One can select a date on which, every month they would like to make the investment, but such monthly amount is usually fixed. Application must be made for a minimum of six months, but one may cancel the SIP anytime they want. Cancellation means, only future instalments of the SIP will not be presented to the investor's bank account. It does not mean that accumulated mutual fund units will be sold too, automatically. To sell or redeem the units, one must place a request to the mutual fund to sell specific number of units or all units or units equivalent to a certain amount as necessary and credit the money to the registered bank account or release a cheque favouring the registered bank account number of the investor. One must understand that there will be tax liability if the units are sold within twelve months from the date of transaction in addition to attracting exit load, which mutual funds charge to discourage short-term selling by investors. For such purposes as exit load and taxes, in case of SIP, each instalment is treated as a separate and individual transaction. In case of lump sum, one can invest a minimum of Rs. 5000 and in case of SIP, as low as Rs. 100 per month can be invested, subject to initial long-term commitment (to continue the SIP). Under the same folio in which a SIP is active, one can make random lump sum investments as and when they please, without creating a new folio. This does not affect the SIP continuity. Moreover, all transactions made in various schemes of a mutual fund can be tracked through a single statement if they are under one folio.

Various fundamental and technical aspects of fund selection that have been discussed above are available in the periodic fund factsheets published by mutual funds. Investors must be sure to read them or seek such information from their advisers and take informed decisions before investing. Reader may also note that the NAV published by mutual funds are final i.e. net of all expenses and charges, which means you get what you see. Whatever Total Expense Ratio (TER) is charged by the scheme is adjusted before publishing the NAV. Hence, for example, if return as per NAV is 12%, it is 12% final without any other adjustments unless there is an exit load in individual cases of redemptions or switches within twelve months from the investment date.

In Indian mutual fund industry, today two types of plans exist under each scheme viz. Direct and Regular. The portfolio and the management of both plans are same, but the difference exists in the financials because of the difference between the expense ratios as per the regulations of SEBI. Hence, the NAV of direct plans is higher than that of regular plans. To distribute direct plans, a distributor must have registered with SEBI as a Registered Investment Adviser (RIA) under the SEBI Investment Adviser Regulations, 2013. Such advisers do not earn any commission from mutual funds but completely rely on the fee their clients possibly pay. I ask, who is the regulator kidding? If you are an Indian reader, I wonder how much fee you are willing to pay the adviser for mutual fund investment advise every year (yes, recurring) and how much will you pay the financial planner every year for comprehensive advice? Not having faith in the fee payments by their individual clients, the other type of distributors sells only regular plans and earn brokerage from mutual funds. One can invest in direct plans even without going to a distributor. They can directly visit the offices of mutual funds or their registrars and submit their applications or transact from the websites in direct plans of various schemes. Because of this arrangement, returns of direct plans are higher than that of regular plans. But, if you invest directly, you will not get advice from advisers like me or better. So, choose wisely.

Sedentary Second Innings

A great lover of the English cinema and Hollywood, I believe the trend of cinema reflects the trend in the society. As much as I appreciate the philosophy and cultural ascendancy of the West, I dislike the trend of the present and past generations when it comes to family (at least, that is what I have perceived from movies). No sooner the children attain the age of majority or graduate, either they leave the family, or the parents kick them out, only in turn for the parents to live not in solitude in their old, age, but in lack love, care and companionship of their children and grand' that is no better than that of an orphaned destitute . Thankfully, I still live happily with my parents and siblings in spite of our squabbles during family discussions. But I believe my musings are insignificant to the world.

What comes to your mind when you hear the word 'Retirement?' Pension, is it not? Well, that is not your mistake. That is how it has been for years and decades. No sooner than I start talking about retirement in most of the first meetings with my clients (or usually prospects), I get responses such as 'I have done my retirement planning', 'I have a pension plan', and 'I know what you want to say, already.' Though I rarely lose my cool on hearing such responses, I usually pity them. With time, innovative ideas, needs, techniques and methods come our way. Old ways are treated as obsolete as all old people are (modern thought, not mine). Everyone, particularly the elderly, know what needs one has in old age. Yet the needs are ignored generally and those who disregard those needs surely pay a price in their later years. This chapter focuses on such needs, which you may have ignored or even never thought of, or in the least, you thought that no planning was necessary. That is where the financial planner comes into picture. After all, the job of the planner is to help you identify and plan for all the financial needs and goals that occur throughout your lifetime whether you can foresee or not.

Retirement is not merely about pension. There are and can be other financial needs and goals too. If you can recollect, in the chapter on risk management, I made a mention of one such need – the old age medical emergencies. There is no machine or system in the world that constantly fights to keep itself functioning actively and healthy as human body does. Our cells die every second, but the body constantly generates new ones. Perhaps, with passage of time or due to never-ending and tiring struggle, natural rejuvenation of the human body continues at a declining rate, consequently draining vital energies, eventually resulting in an inevitable natural phenomenon we call, old age. If you read the chapter 'Safeguarding the benefits', you would not again argue here that a disciplined life rids us of any adverse health conditions. Those glorious days, if they ever existed are mere fantasies that do not exist now. If one terminal illness or other is possible even at an early age, the probability in old age is so high that it is almost closer to certainty. Overlooking such a need can prove devastating and drill a permanent gigantic hole in the retirement corpus.

Besides old age healthcare, there can be other needs and goals, which in case of some individuals fall due after retirement. While one may have a goal to celebrate the anniversary of togetherness with one's life partner in a cruise destination (which also may be planned), I am referring to needs or more important goals than that, depending on personal circumstances. Uncommon to India, I have come across individuals who married at (or after) the age of fifty and had children when they were expected to be grandparents. Though not at that exact age, marrying late is a reason higher education of children, their marriages and other such needs and goals occur past retirement. Though the trend is changing with some fathers not wanting to plan for any children goals except their education and want to kick them out when they grow up, mostly that is not so. In India, most fathers still feel the responsibility and take care of their children till the latter are well settled in life and probably even after that. While provisioning of such goals is like what we discussed in the goal planning section of the previous chapter, there is a difference in this case. After retirement, income does not continue as in the case of an individual who works for a regular salary, which means no periodic or lump sum investment can be usually made, unless the family is affluent. While that is a setback, another is that one may, after retirement, have reduced tolerance for investment risk and prefer moderately or less risky investments, which means lower returns and higher contributions during the earning phase. Such situations must be planned more carefully.

Thus, after planning for regular income, the next important need one has to address is medical expenses in old age. Do I need to mention how expensive medical treatment in corporate hospitals is (particularly because that is where most of us find rays of hope for cure)? If you are thinking about any other goals now, you should start to plan for them too. With limited money to live after retirement, you suddenly cannot decide in old age that you will go visiting the cruise destinations.

The gay retiree's inner peace

Did you watch the film 'Kung Fu Panda'? In the movie, Master Shifu tries to practice and attain inner peace after he sends the goose to the prison to prevent Tai-lung from escaping and laying waste to the valley. That is the kind of piece (of peace) one achieves in the absence of a fool proof comprehensive retirement plan. True inner peace is different. It is what Shifu feels at the end of the ultimate battle, lying down in the serene jade palace beside Po, even when the later was persistent about getting something to eat. Without persistence through the earning phase of life, without discipline in sticking to the budget, without proper planning and periodic monitoring of the progress, inner peace cannot be achieved. Among various needs of old age, pension planning is the most crucial.

Elixir of Retirement

Pension has another name – Annuity. In India, pension is payable by only two entities – Central or State Government, and any Life Insurance company. Even those who are not in service of the government or any organisation can make arrangement for pension through life insurance companies. The reader must note that pension is only an idea and not a product i.e. any investment that pays equated, regular, periodic payments must be viewed and assumed as a pension plan; not merely what the government or life insurance companies pay. Such a perception expands the scope for diversification, liquidity, tax efficiency and higher average payments. Let us talk about pension plans of life insurance companies.

Life insurance companies offer two types of pension plans viz. Deferred Annuity and Immediate Annuity. Say you are thirty-five and have twenty-five years to retire. How do you get pension right away? You cannot even imagine it, right? One needs to first save money and invest it for long term. Just like any other long-term goal, investment for pension requires patience and dedication if one wants to achieve the goal and not compromise their old age lifestyle. If you invest in a pension plan for some time and at the end of the usually long term, the accumulated corpus gets converted into pension, such a plan is called a deferred annuity plan i.e. your pension is deferred or postponed to give time to the investment to grow to a sizeable amount so that it can compensate you towards your expenses. Alternately, let us suppose you are a pre-retiree or already retired and you need regular income, beginning at once. You have already amassed some corpus for the purpose. The pension plan that you buy for a regular income is the immediate annuity plan.

In a deferred annuity plan, you invest your money for long term until the corpus you need is accumulated that will make regular payments in the future and then shift the corpus to an immediate annuity plan. Such plans usually involve investments in unit linked insurance plans addressed as the ULIP. Though they are usually understood as having entire investment allocated to equity, there are plans that are a combination of debt and equity in different proportions with varying rates of returns. Besides, due to changes in insurance regulations, insurers play it safe to ensure certain minimum guaranteed return on investment. For the purpose, in addition to premium allocation charge, policy administration charge, and fund management charge, an 'investment guarantee charge' is also levied. In these policies that currently have a lock-in period of five years, it is compulsory unlike earlier to convert the maturity or surrender value into an immediate annuity plan at the prevailing rates. Up to one-third of the corpus may be commuted though. One cache here is that there is no exit option in an immediate annuity plan. Once you buy it, it stays forever, subject to chosen options and policy conditions. Moreover, once bought, prevailing interest rate (rate at which annuity is paid on the purchase corpus) will continue for the remaining policy term or life. About twenty years ago (between 1995 and 1998), interest rates used to be as high as 12% per annum. A person aged fifty who bought an immediate annuity plan at that rate for life then, would be receiving pension even today at the same rate when interest rates are as low as 7% and will continue to receive 12% (God bless him!) for another twenty years or more by when the rates might fall to as low as 4%. The question here is, 'do you want to lock your money at the prevailing interest rate, for the rest of your life?' If the current interest rates compared to the future expectation are so high, why not? There is yet another challenge to be addressed. Pension in India is taxable just like salary or business incomes. However, the tax rates for senior citizens are presently liberal. For someone who has an income up to Rs. 5 Lakhs per annum, the effective tax rate is as low as 2%. Those who yearn precision in everything may include this 2% in the calculations while deriving the required retirement corpus if they can foresee or estimate the possibility of the present tax benefits continuing in the future. Immediate annuity plans usually have a few options for buyers to choose from. The most common option is 'annuity for life' i.e. annuity or pension is paid to the buyer or policy holder throughout his or her lifetime. The pension stops with the death of the buyer. In this option, the annuity amount is the highest comparatively. Second is the joint life option in which annuity is paid to the last survivor when taken on the joint lives of husband and wife. Third is increasing annuity option i.e. the pension amount increases every year, throughout the policy term, at 3% to 5% to counter the inflation effect. In the case of life annuity or joint life options, an addition can be made for returning the purchase price or principal amount to the legal heirs. In such a case, the monthly or periodic annuity payment made to the buyer would be significantly lower. One should compare the annuity payments under diverse options before settling on one.

Let us take this an example and understand how one should go about it. Always curious and intrigued, wondering if there have been any changes in the crucial attributes of these plans, I have done some research and evaluated a few of them. I say, nothing has changed. Regulations mandate that benefit illustrations of life insurance policies show performance calculations at two estimated rates – 8% and 4%. I liberally went by 8% return and did the workings. Let us see the example. Suppose you invest Rs. 1 Lakh every year, for thirty years, expecting a return of 8% per annum. At the end of the period, your corpus should be 1.22 Crore. However, the benefit illustration of a life insurance company showed a maturity value (depending on market performance and the charges levied) of approx. Rs. 50 Lakhs. I calculated the return and it turned out to be 3.12% per annum. I checked the past performance of the underlying product and the return for the last five years was close to 8% per annum. Yet, the benefit illustration showed a maturity value that calculates to a meagre 3.12% comparatively. Not drawing any conclusions quickly, I verified a policy of another insurer and found that against 8% expected return, the benefit illustration showed a maturity value that calculated to only 5.67%. Of course, the 8% and 4% shown in benefit illustration are indicative only, and do not represent actual performance, which depends on several factors. If actual return is, say, 15% and 3% or 5% goes towards management expenses of the company and we are left with 10% or 12% that will still help us in comfortably achieving our goal, there is nothing wrong in the experienced and efficient professional charging us a reasonable fee. The problem arises when returns are meagre, below expectation and yet the fund levies charges, taking overall return further down. These are some of the reasons why, despite strong, supporting arguments made by insurance professionals, advisers across the globe largely express aversion to investment plans managed by life insurance companies that combine investment and insurance.

Nevertheless, if one desires regular pension, one may go ahead and buy an immediate annuity plan. But, one need not (I am not saying 'must not') buy a deferred annuity plan if the goal is due many years hence. Besides, once a deferred annuity plan is started, there is no turning back. The new regulations make it compulsory to convert it into an immediate annuity plan at maturity. Hence, it is only logical not to act out of impulse but evaluate various alternatives, as accumulation can be done through any financial product. Once the accumulation phase comes to an end, one can decide whether to put entire retirement corpus in an immediate annuity plan or divide it among various products (for distinct reasons).

If not the pension plans of life insurance companies, where else can you invest? Well, mutual funds are an appropriate choice. Depending on the asset allocation, you may choose equity or hybrid or debt funds. Until a decade ago, the good old products used to be categorised as Defined Benefit and Defined Contribution plans. Though such features exist even today, the perception has changed. If one has enough principal to sufficiently diversify, even direct equity is an option. On the conservative side, there are avenues such as the Public Provident Fund and the National Pension System. Wherever you invest, you must ensure that the return from the product matches the requirement. Let us understand how to plan for retirement, from an example.

After struggling with the numbers, suppose you have listed all your expenses – recurring and infrequent and settled at an annual expenditure of Rs. 5 Lakhs. You are now forty and intend to retire at sixty-five. You want to have an annuity for twenty years after retirement. At an estimated average inflation of 5% that is constant for the remainder of life, your current expenses of Rs. 5 Lakhs will inflate to Rs. 17 Lakhs per annum by the time you retire. Assuming a moderate return of 7% on investment post-retirement, to be able to meet those ever-rising expenses for another twenty years, at retirement you will have to have a corpus of Rs. 2.85 Crores that you will have to create in twenty-five years.

Supposing you have a moderately-aggressive investment risk profile and a relative rate of return of 11% per annum, your net monthly investment requirement comes to Rs. 19000, ignoring any taxes on maturity or redeeming the investment. This amount may now be divided among various asset classes and held until the goal year. You may apply the strategies you learnt in Goal Planning section of the previous chapter here too.

A prudent financial planner suggests the better way between the above and this. In the above example, you have a corpus requirement of Rs. 2.85 Crores, for which you need to invest Rs. 19000 per month that you must divide among the three asset classes. Now, let us see how it turns out, in the below table.

Asset Class	Allocation	Return	Weighted	Invest p.m.	Future Value
Equity	75%	12.00%	9.00%	14250	2.55 Crores
Debt	20%	8.50%	1.70%	3800	0.39 Crores
Gold	5%	6.00%	0.30%	950	0.06 Crores
Net Return			11.00%	19000	3.00 Crores

If you divide the monthly investible amount of Rs. 19000 as per the asset allocation, monthly investments made in equity, debt and gold in the given proportions will create a corpus of Rs. 3.00 Crores, whereas your requirement is only 2.85 Crores. You may argue that Rs. 15 Lakhs in such long term is not much significant and it is okay. But it is not about mere 15 Lakhs that are in today's value (discounted with inflation rate) Rs. 4.43 Lakhs ($6300). It is about knowing various strategies, evaluating them, and choosing the appropriate one. If you liberally allow a planner to take a deviation once, he might take liberty and deviate from the ideal method in the case of some critical need, without your knowledge. Your future need is Rs. 2.85 Crores. Instead of calculating the investible amount of Rs. 19000 per month, divide Rs. 2.85 Crores as per asset allocation and then calculate the investible amounts for equity, debt, and gold separately. The below table highlights the contrast between the previous table and this strategy.

Asset Class	Allocation	Inflated Cost	Return	Invest p.m.	Future Value
Equity	75%	21375000	12.00%	11900	21320000
Debt	20%	5700000	8.50%	5600	5740000
Gold	5%	1425000	6.00%	2000	1400000
Total	100%	28500000	10.75%	19500	28460000

The minor difference in the corpus has occurred due to rounding-off of the monthly investible amounts to the nearest hundred (as we are not used to investing to the last rupee and paisa) over a long term of twenty-five years. In this method, the return calculates to only 10.75% and the investible amount goes up by Rs. 500 ($ 7) a month. Choosing between the two methods of calculation depends on what is appropriate and on the other hand, will your cashflows allow another five hundred to be invested or not.

Let us consider another scenario. Suppose your current cashflow does not allow you to invest Rs. 19000 per month after allocating for various insurance plans and loan instalments. Say you have a discretionary cashflow of just

10000 per month but that is not an impossible barrier. As your income increases year on year, you need to keep increasing the investments by a thousand or two like 11000 in the second year, 13000 in the third year, 15000 in the fourth year and so on. These increments must continue even after the originally calculated amount of Rs. 19500 has been reached, so as to compensate the loss of compounding effect during the years when amounts lower than 19500 were invested.

Reverse Mortgage

In the vastness of population such as India's, though the percentage may be less, the number of families deprived of a steady and reasonable income in the middle and old ages is depressingly high. There are older couples that invested their life savings for the future of their children who abandoned their parents to pursue their own dreams in the glittering-West, those that do not have an offspring to care for them in their later years, and those who have their loving yet financially impossible progeny living with them (ignoring countless varieties of dreadful tales of bereaved souls that cannot be emancipated) – all lacking a secured stream of regular income. Some are fortunate to have created assets like an interest-yielding bank deposit and a house. On one hand the interest income may be inadequate and on the other, the property does not add to the cashflows as it is not let out for rent. Studies and innovations in the world of financial services lead to the evolution of a banking product that addresses this gap, which is called Reverse Mortgage.

In the simplest terms, a reverse mortgage is a loan. While in a regular mortgage of a house property the borrower receives lump sum amount and repays the lender (usually a bank) through equated monthly instalments, the opposite happens in a reverse mortgage. After mortgaging the property, rather than paying the instalments, the borrower who should be at least sixty years old receives instalments from the lending bank for a certain number of years. While receiving the income, the owner can continue to live in the house. In fact, this loan is released only on the property that is self-occupied by the owners. The maximum period for which the lender pays instalment income, is fifteen years. However, some banks may extend it to twenty. In either case, the expected future life of the property must be at least twenty years. Normally, longer the loan tenure, lower is the instalment income paid to the borrower. As per the guidelines stipulated by the Reserve Bank of India, the loan amount based on which the instalment amount is decided, should not exceed 60% of the value of the property. Before processing the loan, the lending bank evaluates the property based on a range of factors including the age, condition, geographical location, and the market value for a similar property in the area etc. For example, if a loan of Rs. 10 Lakhs is approved, the monthly income calculates to Rs. 11000 at 12% rate of interest for a twenty-year tenure. The mortgage terminates at the end of the fifteen or twenty-year period or when the last borrower dies. The mortgage may be closed during the tenure by repaying the bank the loan availed until that point, along with any other charges the bank may impose. However, I believe such situation may not arise because if one has the financial ability to repay, one would not opt for a such a loan in the first place. Upon the death or the completion of the term, the owner or the legal heirs are given an option to repay the loan amount and retain the house. If neither the surviving borrower nor the heirs are either unwilling or unable to repay the loan, the property is sold by the bank. If the sale proceeds exceed the amount of loan over such a long tenure, the lender returns the difference. In the unfortunate event that the sale proceeds are insufficient to close the loan, the bank bears the loss but not burden borrower.

While I have seen and read about struggling families who have the means yet reluctant to accept the available solution, one such instance occurred in my own close circle. A man died a miserable death holding too much sentiment to the property, while he struggled to make ends meet when he lived, which eventually led to his early departure and his widow retreating to live at the mercy of her relatives. The man could not take his possessions to his after-life nor can the old woman enjoy the material, while she was deprived of what was truly precious to her. Reverse mortgage is certainly not for those, who despite their financial hurdles desire a tragic life. It is for those who want to make a difference and give something back to their fellow-men through their experience and wisdom, while they are not merely alive but living an ideal life.

Employee Benefits

In insurance, there are two ways to protect oneself from pecuniary loss – buy insurance or go for self-insurance i.e. create a corpus and take precautions such as installing fire extinguishers, exercising for health, acquiring new and contemporary skills etc. Similarly, when it comes to retirement planning, old age income is not completely left to individuals. For those who are in service or employment of the government or private sector, there are diverse benefits that can add to the nest egg of employees. If managed carefully, these benefits make significant contribution to the retirement corpus. However, these contributions take long years to grow, given the typically low amounts of contributions or the provisions of various laws that govern them. Such types of benefits certainly do not suit the present and future generations of employees who cannot upgrade their skills constantly and stay loyal to their masters. Two such benefits that we shall see here are Gratuity and Provident Fund.

Gratuity: It is paid to an employee leaving the service through retirement or resignation or termination including layoff except for fraudulent activities or upon death of the employee, to the legal heirs. It is a defined benefit plan that came into force with the passing of the Payment of Gratuity Act, 1972. Gratuity is payable to employees that leave service after they have put in at least five years of continuous service. However, in the unfortunate event of death of an employee, the minimum five years of service rule is exempted. Any establishment that has ten or more employees, comes under the purview of the Act. Even if the number of employees falls below ten at any later stage, once an establishment comes under the Act, it will continue to be governed by the Act i.e. the employer must pay gratuity irrespective of the number of employees. The Act has specified a formula for calculating the gratuity payable. It is defined as 'half-month salary for every completed year of service' i.e. for every year of service that an individual has put, fifteen days salary is paid as gratuity. For the purpose, salary includes basic pay and dearness allowance drawn by the employee at the time of leaving the service. As regards the years of service, in the last year, a service of six months or more is treated as a full year.

Let us take an example. An individual joined the service of a private company in 2010 for a monthly basic salary of Rs. 10000, when he was barely twenty-five. He retires from service in 2045, at the age of 60. Over the thirty-five years, at an average rate of 5% per annum, his basic salary increased to Rs. 55000 at retirement. As per the defined benefit formula, the employee is entitled for a minimum gratuity of Rs. 11 Lakhs. Is that not sweet?! Besides, the employee has not contributed as single rupee to the fund. How many individuals who are in service and prefer their own investments and disregard gratuity, made investments out of the extra income they gained from switching jobs that will make this addition to the retirement corpus?

Provident Fund: Contributions to the provident fund for employees, is governed by the Employees Provident Fund and Miscellaneous Provisions Act, 1952. An establishment that has twenty or more employees, in addition to certain other conditions stipulated by the Act, gets covered under the Act. Once an establishment is covered, it remains covered forever. Usually, employees who draw a basic salary of Rs. 15000 or less at the time of joining are eligible to become member of the fund. However, in the case of employees drawing basic salary of more than the stipulated amount, their membership to the fund is conditional. As per the Act, the employee contributes 12% of his basic pay and the employer makes equal contribution to the fund. However, the entire contribution does not go to provident fund. Under the Act, there are three schemes viz. Employees Provident Fund, Employees' Pension Scheme and Employees Deposit Linked Insurance. The 12% contribution of the employee completely goes to the provident fund account whereas as only 3.67% of the employer's contribution goes to provident fund while the rest 8.33% goes to the pension scheme. In case of employees earning more than 15000 basic pay, even though they get covered under the Act, the employer's contribution is limited only to 12% of Rs. 15000 while the employee can contribute more than 12%. Provident fund withdrawn before putting in a minimum of five years of continuous service attracts tax liability. Hence, one must be cautious about redeeming the fund. Apportioning it to the retirement goal and sticking to it helps building the retirement corpus sooner or reduces the strain thereby making allowances to plan for other goals. Let us see an example. Suppose an individual joined service at the age of thirty, with a basic salary of Rs. 15000. Assuming the basic salary grows at a conservative rate of 3% per annum to Rs. 35000 over the next thirty years of earning phase, the employer's standard contribution of 12% on 15000 aggregates to Rs. 6.48 Lakhs before interest, irrespective of 3% increase, while the employee's contribution cumulates to Rs. 10 Lakhs. At retirement, the total contributions along with interest at an average interest of 8% per annum will grow to Rs. 57 Lakhs. Even if the employee's own contribution of 12% to provident fund is disregarded, the employer's contribution is valued at Rs. 25 Lakhs at the time of retirement, provided no intermittent withdrawals have been made from the fund during the course of service. In addition to the employer's and employee's contributions, the central government contributes 1.67% of Rs. 15000 basic salary to the pension scheme.

Delayed Expenditure

While working the budget for retirement, one must be sure not to include expenses like children education costs, support to parents, loan instalments, insurance premiums etc. The reason to exclude these expenses is that, usually during the post-retirement phase, the kids will be independent, and your loans and policies will have by and large, matured. Another important thing to note is that the expenses you think you will incur at retirement should be in present value and as per the expected lifestyle post-retirement. For example, if you are spending 1000 per month on health care (does not mean just medicines) today, assuming you are retired, in today's value, you may spend 3000 per month. This is because of the increased risk at that age. And if you are spending 20000 per month on groceries and utilities, in old age, since the kids will be independent, you may plan to spend less comparatively. So, you may cut down your lifestyle expenses to 15000.

While retirement planning can be started as early as the beginning of one's career, one must prepare for the opening of a new chapter in their life, least a year or two before retirement. Some say retirement is a never-ending vacation, others call it the beginning of the end, while some other say different. In real, retirement can be anything one wants it to be. In India, it is perhaps an instinct but of all pre-retirees, those that serve the government or public sector undertakings are more calculative and cautious, busy preparing for their later years, as they get closer to their retirement. Having almost fixed pay scales that are pre-defined until the termination of service, they know how much they will receive in the name of gratuity, provident fund or annuity and the applicable taxes on such proceeds. Though it is a good thing to be aware of one's defined benefits, there are other things to do in addition to calculating the corpus or reviewing financial goals. You should check how expenses have inflated and how your lifestyle has changed over the years. And, since you are close to retirement, you have a better idea of what your post-retirement expenses will be. Let me explain. When you first planned at 30, you projected that your then expenses of 30000 per month would inflate to 1.60 Lakhs. However, at 55 when you checked your expenses, you found yourself spending 2 Lakhs a month. The reason obviously is inflation but the higher-than-expected rise in expenses can be due to the improved lifestyle. In the beginning, you thought you would spend the same amount (adjusted for inflation) at 55 that you were spending at 30. However, early progress in your career changed your lifestyle too. And now, accustomed to your improved lifestyle, you may find it difficult to compromise on your expenses in old age. So, you need to rework the budget you proposed for post-retirement life and see how far the proposed retirement corpus will support you in meeting the old age expenses. If there is any chance, you may try to recoup the difference during the last few years of earning phase.

Old Age Care

In continuation to the discussion on terminal illness in the chapter on insurance and risk management, let us address the healthcare expenditure incurred in the old age, naturally post-retirement. Let us say a man retired at 60 and received retirement proceeds of 50 Lakhs, all sources combined. Seven years past retirement, the man suffers from critical health issues and is hospitalised. Due to constant digging into the fund towards monthly expenses for which it was meant, the corpus has already depreciated to Rs. 35 Lakhs. He gets great treatment in a private hospital and recovers faster. But after spending Rs. 10 Lakhs on treatment that the doctors called complicated, his corpus is down to 25 Lakhs. Additionally, monthly outflow has increased by 5000/-, which is spent towards medicines and health care. Now he spends 35000 per month instead of 30000 before hospitalization, while the corpus is down on the other hand. With increased expenses and high-cost medical treatment, the remaining retirement corpus will support him till the age of 73. If fortunately, his disciplined and healthy life style prolongs his longevity to 85 years, how will he survive for more than a decade without any income? He will have to depend on his children for daily needs and you do not know where they are and what they are, as is the experience at present times.

You may be thinking that I have forgotten about health insurance. Well, I have not. Health related expenses are an integral part of both risk management and retirement planning and ignoring them is just short of a sin. Let us understand through an example. Today, let us suppose a 55-60-year-old person must pay a premium of 40000 for health insurance cover of 5 Lakhs. By the time a 30-year-old person retires at 58 in the next 28 years, the premium will have inflated significantly. Also, you cannot say that 5 Lakhs in present value will be enough even after 28 years, can you? With the advancements in medical world & technology, today, doctors do anything to keep us not just alive but healthy too. Before we are allowed to pass, our wealth is dried out to the last penny, but we are ensured good health and long life, unless fate decides otherwise. Let us assume the expenses in medical world increase at a higher rate than the household expenses i.e. inflation in health care industry is more than general and food inflation. Accordingly, the current requirement of 5 Lakhs towards medical expenses will inflate to 75 Lakhs in 28 years and the premium too will rise to Rs. 6 Lakhs.

No one suddenly falls ill the moment they retire. A person who led an active life for 30-35 years does not immediately fall sick and is hospitalized merely because he has retired. Because of his years of active life, he will adopt new activities or pick up a hobby and adapt to new life style. Now, imagine for few years say, until 65, he has not had any need for insurance i.e. from 58 when he retired until 65, for 7 years nothing happened. To keep the policy in force, he will have to pay premiums of Rs. 6 Lakhs per annum aggregating to Rs. 42 Lakhs in seven years. Since this is not an investment, the premium paid is gone (though the risk is insured for that period). And, how did the person afford that much premium? It is the retirement corpus that he received from various sources over decades of earning phase. So, in old age, particularly after retirement, do you want to buy health insurance or create a corpus? The difference is, unlike in health insurance, if you create a corpus to meet medical expenses in old age and you do not contract any major illness, your money stays with you. If you need it, you always have it ready. And if you do not need it, it will continue to grow at least at risk-free rate. Which of the two options do you choose - create corpus of 75 Lakhs and keep your hard-earned money with you or buy health insurance and pay 42 Lakhs premium for a cover of 75 Lakhs? When I say the above, I am not implying that no hospitalisation need arises from age 58 till 65 or before. It is merely an example to explain you the difference between growing corpus the cost of growing health insurance premium, and help you take a better decision.

With changing times, healthcare needs are taking a new turn. Domiciliary hospitalisation (healthcare and treatment at home), which has been mostly in theory, has been gaining prominence of late. Demand for such services as nursing, diagnosis etc. at one's house is increasing gradually. One should consider provisioning for such expenses in old age, in addition to medical emergency fund or health insurance.

Retreat to serenity

Once your key requirement of post-retirement life i.e. continued cash inflow has been setup, it is time to look at other goals. For one, how did you picture your old age life style? Do you wish to live in a bird's nest kind of apartment in a skyscraper in the concrete jungle, in the heart of a metropolis where you can breathe pollution (a compromise for enjoying modern amenities) or, do you yearn to live in a house in a serene county with some good space around, where there's less noise, where you can breathe fresh air, relax in the lawn, grow some flowers and vegetables in the yard etc., but within the proximity of community centres like hospitals in case of emergencies? Which sounds better to you? Well, if you prefer the former or if you already have a beautiful house, I do not have anything to say but otherwise, you need to plan for things in an orderly fashion. Though this is part of a broader financial planning exercise, it also forms part of retirement planning.

Suppose you want to live in a house when you retire and the estimated cost of the house in today's value is 50 Lakhs in a secluded place. You presently own and live in an apartment that is valued at 30 Lakhs at present market rate. Observe that the price and place are both different. Assuming the property prices inflate or grow at 5% per annum, in 30 years, the cost of the house property you propose to move to will be 2.15 Crores. If you consider disposing off the apartment to fund the house purchase goal, you will receive a sum of 1.30 Crore only, leaving a gap of 85 Lakhs. If you do not plan and account for this at an early stage, you will have to compromise on your lifestyle in old age.

The figure may seem scary but do not worry. If you start planning for this deficit at an early age when you planned for retirement say, 30, in a high-risk high-return portfolio, you will have to invest just 3000 per month. Suppose you ignore this for five years. You will have to invest 5500 per month till you retire. And unfortunately, if you do not realise the need to plan for this deficit till you are 40, you will need to shell out 10000 per month for the remainder of your earning phase. Which do you think is more convenient, a comfortable 3000 per month or a worrisome 10000 per month? All figures given in examples are only indicative and must not be considered as they are. For all practical purposes, you should consult a financial planner or if you are planning yourself, take a calculated decision.

Leaving a legacy behind

What is the purpose of life? It is a subjective question that opens doors for never-ending discussion. Perhaps if spiritual side of the question is ignored, the purpose of life is what one likes to do with it (their own life, not with that of others). One may want to make significant contributions to mathematical and scientific, another may want to revolutionise agricultural practices, some other may want to change the society and leave their mark on the coming generations. Majority are content with what they have, and the rest may have no clue about their future. But what is legacy? It is something that you pass on to the next generations, be it wisdom or riches or both that will be remembered and cherished for a long time. Legacy need not be as grand as that of Aryabhatta, Patanjali and Aristotle of the ancient times, who are celebrated even to this day or that of Isaac Newton, Albert Einstein, Mother Teresa, and Gandhi in the new age. It can be as simple as taking care of one's family and fulfilling their responsibilities to the family and society in one's own capacity, setting examples to the closely observing younger generation to follow in respect and admiration. The young certainly and the middle-aged perhaps do not understand but the old does know how it feels to have grandchildren, raise them, play with them, buy them stuff, tell them stories, and teach them right and wrong and defend them from their strict parents. The older they grow, the more they care and the more they love, the more they want to pass on – in the present times, not values or age-old traditions but material wealth. After all, in the present when everyone openly calls themselves wise, motivating, knowing-all, thinkers and assume such other fancy terms besides literally boasting that they *can give a lot of 'gyan'* (meaning, wisdom), the only thing that holds real value in the material world is money, that which the majority lack and those that have it not share.

Love, Money, and Wisdom

People who say that money does not bring happiness are two types – those that already have amassed enough wealth, and those that do not have money or the vision and desperation to earn it beyond their necessities. I do not want to argue with the wise men who say one need not have money to be happy. This book is not for such wise, who are far above the material needs of present modern age when smartphones, social networking and selfies are inseparable from daily lives. I bow before them in awe and touch their feet. I remember saying this sometime back on some social networking site. *'Money does bring happiness, but money is not the only thing that brings happiness, all the time'*. This holds key to a fulfilling life before and after retirement. One may want to jog or run for health, but the dense smog of the over-populous metropolis may be seriously discouraging after a few days. Buying a pair of running shoes, a treadmill, and an air purifier to run indoors costs so much money that can equal the yearly living expenses of a small family in India. One may be desirous of learning music or playing an instrument, but a professional trainer and the instrument do not come as charity. Besides, such expenses may be of recurring nature though the frequency can vary. One must love and yearn to earn money beyond the necessities so as to not sacrifice such petty desires and hobbies. But one must be wary that the love for money never supersedes the love and attention for the family and fellow-men. Money is so inseparable from life that at times, it may not be an exaggeration to say that wisdom can depend on financial independence. One may gain subject matter expertise relating to their profession from experience over time. But that is not the same as wisdom. To be looked to for advice and wisdom, one may have to read books on diverse subjects, learn languages and arts, debate with learned communities, travel the world, understand geographies, lifestyles, and cultures, gaze into space, watch world movies, play sports and it never ends. Without a regular stream of low-risk or no-risk cash inflows in the form interest or dividend to depend on, today it is humanly not possible to pursue one is such dreams of learning. Partial knowledge or information acquired through internet search may prove dangerous at times. What we pass on to the next generation, how they treat us and how we lead our life also form part of comprehensive financial planning. Bequeathing an estate is an integral part of the planning process and requires special understanding of the subject and expertise.

Laws of succession

'What is more beautiful than Death?' – a dialogue from the film Clash of the Titans, it is a philosophy of the highest order not understandable, digestible, and cherished by many. I envy Hollywood for its greatness. If any culture can embrace death so naturally, Indians have it first in their blood and genes. Yet, as I said in the chapter 'Safeguarding the benefits', death is the most unsavoury subject that advisers shun from discussing and their clients from hearing it, despite both being constantly aware of its inevitability. With growing age, people open up about it more often, when it is too late to make any amendments. In the modern West, while making a financial plan, among the needs and goals, there is one that financial planners mention that is unorthodox to India – creating a reserve for one's own funeral expenses. When a financial planner made this suggestion on their Twitter account few years ago, I was so furious that I replied *'It might hold true to the West. But in India, if a person has to pay for his own funeral, may the family be dead!'* and I stick to the comment forever. In the US, funeral expenses might be around $ 10000, which convert to 7 Lakhs in Indian Rupees. While a regular ritual is not usually cheap, Rs. 7 Lakhs certainly gives a pinch for the middle-class household while it can be a pinch for the affluent but boastful. For someone who wants it to be a grandeur, if the ritual goes by the book in the present times, the expenditure may even cross a million (rupees, not dollars). So, when I rejected the idea of making provisions for funeral expenses, I meant it for an individual planning for his own funeral to not burden his children or even due to lack of faith in them. I suggest though that the children, devoid of sentiment but out of love for their parents, add the expenditure as a financial goal in the plan. On the contrary, an Indian should if he so desires, focus on leaving an estate for his posterity, which can cushion the latter's personal finances and wellbeing.

How do you ensure that after your lifetime, your estate i.e. fixed or financial assets and everything else goes to your spouse or children for sure? You may be thinking, 'if not to them, who else will it go to?' Since the evolution of judicial system, succession has been one of the most contested categories of civil suits in India. Whether or not the immediate family members are true heirs, even a false suit filed in an Indian court of law can slog for a decade or sometimes a lifetime before the rightful ones win it, depriving them of the estate and benefits therefrom that may seem, forever. It is a practice in India that while opening a bank account or proposing a life insurance plan or making an investment, people register one or more nominees who may be family members or a relative or some other person, expecting them to receive that money in the event of their untimely passing. What one does not know is that the nominee(s) will have to handover the estate to the legal heirs, unless they are themselves the legal heirs. It is only that when nominees are legal heirs, transfer of property becomes easier. One can only imagine what may happen if a person does not assign or register a nominee for various assets.

When one thinks of bequeathing one's estate, it is always best to write a 'Will'. It is a common misbelief that will is a document for the well-off or someone who has triggered a certain age. In fact, any individual who is of the age of majority i.e. 18 years or older, can write a will. And not just property, jewels, and valuables but even items that hold sentimental value to the near and dear can be mentioned in the will, like art, antiquities, instruments, ornaments etc. Even more, modern, digital assets such as a website and an email account can be bequeathed if one so wishes. After all, it is your Will! The Testator who writes the will need not register it. Registration of the will is called Probate. If you are writing the will on your own without professional help, be sure to be very lucid and particular in your writing. Ambiguous will can prove costly to legal heirs and discouraging, thereby defeating the very purpose it is meant to address. A will supersedes all nominations whatsoever and the latest or newest will replaces all the earlier ones. However, in the case of insurance policies, as per the provisions of the Insurance Act, 1938, the insurer pays the claim proceeds to the nominees. It is up to the legal heirs (if they are different from nominee) to contest and takeover the funds from the nominee. Hence, one should recheck the nominations one made and make changes if necessary, despite writing a will. Some even suggest creating a Trust on paper to ensure the heirs are not deprived of the estate. Consulting a legal adviser or a tax consultant or an estate planner in such cases is advisable.

When one dies without a will, it is called dying intestate. What happens then? How is the estate distributed among the legal heirs? Information in this part has been taken from the Hindu Succession Act, 1956. *The act names legal heirs in two classes. The Class I heirs in the case of a Hindu male are son; daughter; widow; mother; son of a predeceased son; daughter of a predeceased son; son of a predeceased daughter; daughter of a predeceased daughter; widow of a predeceased son; son of a predeceased son of a predeceased son; daughter of a predeceased son of a predeceased son; widow of a predeceased son of a predeceased son. In the absence of any class I heirs, the property devolves on class II heirs, who are as follows – 1. Father; 2. Son's daughter's son, son's daughter's daughter, brother, sister; 3. Daughter's son's son, daughter's son's daughter, daughter's daughter's son, daughter's daughter's daughter; 4. Brother's son, sister's son, brother's daughter, sister's daughter; 5. Father's father, father's mother; 6. Father's widow, brother's widow; 7. Father's brother, father's sister; 8. Mother's father, mother's mother; 9. Mother's brother, mother's sister. A person is said to be an Agnate of the other, if the two are related by blood or adoption wholly through males. A person is said to be a Cognate of the other, if the two are related by blood or adoption but not wholly through males. The property of a male Hindu dying intestate shall devolve according to the provisions of Chapter II of the Act which are — (a) firstly, upon the heirs, being the relatives specified in class I of the Schedule; (b) secondly, if there is no heir of class I, then upon the heirs, being the relatives specified in class II of the Schedule; (c) thirdly, if there is no heir of any of the two classes, then upon the agnates of the deceased; and (d) lastly, if there is no agnate, then upon the cognates of the deceased. Among the heirs specified, those in class I shall take simultaneously and to the exclusion of all other heirs; those in the first entry in class II shall be preferred to those in the second entry; those in the second entry shall be preferred to those in the third entry; and so on in succession.* Additional rules have been specified in the Act that define the share of each of the class I heirs. A 2005 amendment to the Act gives equal rights to daughters, like that of sons in case of ancestral property, after the death of the father. The laws of succession applicable to Christians and Muslims are a different subject for a different time. I suggest the reader to refer and thoroughly understand the full Act along with any amendments made till date or consult a professional before arriving at a conclusion to avoid financial or other losses and disappointments.

Taxing Social Responsibilities

Taxes are taxing. They are unpleasant to hear, read about and pay. Do you remember the scene in the movie 'Avengers' when Loki seizes the Tesseract from Nick Fury? In response to Fury's statement, Loki gives an epic reply – 'an ant has no argument with a boot'. In spite of having a net taxable income above the basic exemption limit, that is how some families may feel when they are compelled by law to pay tax on their income, while they are neck-deep in debt and burdened with personal financial obligations. Of course, it is impossible for any government to investigate personal financial positions of each tax assessee and make suitable provisions that will appease them. For that reason, the government has made provisions through various sections of the Income Tax Act, which can help tax payers reduce or eliminate their tax liability through exemption and deduction benefits, up to a reasonable level. Utilising these provisions allowed by the Act to the best possible extent to reduce once tax liability is called Tax Planning. Though initially it may appear legal, identifying any loopholes in law in a manipulative fashion and escaping tax liability is regarded as Tax Avoidance. Deliberately avoiding or ignoring to pay tax despite one's net liability is called Tax Evasion and treated as a felony. As a responsible Indian, we are concerned only with tax planning. I already said that I intend to keep this book timeless, which is why I shall not discuss certain aspects of taxation such as the individual income tax slabs or provisions that may change every year or expected to change in the near future or short term. We shall focus more on the qualitative side of taxation. One who studies tax laws and understands the essence of taxation knows that it is not an impossible subject. One who can apply common sense, understand, and avoid possibilities of 'undue advantage' that may lead to extra benefit and thrill to the assessee, can understand the rules of income tax well and make use of relevant sections for tax planning. After all, income tax rules have been framed by the learned but humans with great common sense. It is not rocket-science or advance mathematics of another world. ***In this chapter, information relating to taxes has been sourced from the website of Income Tax department of India.***

[It is a matter of general belief that taxes on income and wealth are of recent origin but there is enough evidence to show that taxes on income in some form or the other were levied even in primitive and ancient communities. The origin of the word "Tax" is from "Taxation" which means an estimate. These were levied either on the sale and purchase of merchandise or livestock and were collected in a haphazard manner from time to time. Nearly 2000 years ago, there went out a decree from Ceaser Augustus that all the world should be taxed. In Greece, Germany and Roman Empires, taxes were also levied sometimes based on turnover and sometimes on occupations. For many centuries, revenue from taxes went to the Monarch. In Northern England, taxes were levied on land and on moveable property such as the Saladin title in 1188. Later, these were supplemented by introduction of poll taxes, and indirect taxes known as "Ancient Customs" which were duties on wool, leather, and hides. These levies and taxes in various forms and on various commodities and professions were imposed to meet the needs of the Governments to meet their military and civil expenditure and not only to ensure safety to the subjects but also to meet the common needs of the citizens like maintenance of roads, administration of justice and such other functions of the State.

In India, the system of direct taxation as it is known today, has been in force in one form or another even from ancient times. There are references both in Manu Smriti and Arthasastra to a variety of tax measures. Manu, the ancient sage and law-giver stated that the king could levy taxes, according to Sastras. The wise sage advised that taxes should be related to the income and expenditure of the subject. He, however, cautioned the king against excessive taxation and stated that both extremes should be avoided namely either complete absence of taxes or exorbitant taxation. According to him, the king should arrange the collection of taxes in such a manner that the subjects did not feel the pinch of paying taxes. He laid down that traders and artisans should pay $1/5^{th}$ of their profits in silver and gold, while the agriculturists were to pay $1/6^{th}$, $1/8^{th}$ and $1/10^{th}$ of their produce depending upon their circumstances. The detailed analysis given by Manu on the subject clearly shows the existence of a well-planned taxation system, even in ancient times. Not only this, taxes were also levied on various classes of people like actors, dancers, singers and even dancing girls. Taxes were paid in the shape of gold-coins, cattle, grains, raw-materials and by rendering personal service. However, it is Kautilya's Arthasastra, which deals with the system of taxation in an elaborate and planned manner. This well-known treatise on state crafts written sometime in 300 B.C., when the Mauryan Empire was as its glorious upwards move, is amazing for its deep study of the civilisation of that time and the suggestions given which should guide a king in running the State in a most efficient and fruitful manner.

In the present day, The Income Tax Act 1961 lays down the frame work or the basis of charge and the computation of total income of a person. It also stipulates the way it is to be brought to tax, defining in detail the exemptions, deductions, rebates, and reliefs. The Income Tax Department functions under supervision and control of the Central Board of Direct Taxes (CBDT). The Central Board of Direct Taxes is a statutory authority functioning under the Central Board of Revenue Act, 1963. The officials of the Board in their ex-officio capacity also function as a division of the Ministry of Finance, dealing with matters relating to levy and collection of direct taxes.]

Obligated social responsibility

Yes, tax is a social obligation. Whenever an adviser or an economist tries to put sense to the opposing mind, it is common that the latter, the uneducated (not illiterate) rejects the argument by pulling in social evils such as frauds and corruption into the discussion. Notwithstanding that, taxes are building blocks of any nation's economy, defence, infrastructure, and its people's comprehensive welfare. Contributing to this pool through taxes regardless of the amount is something one must cherish and feel proud about but, without unduly demanding and protesting beyond what the government is already reasonably providing except when such provisions are not productive. The next time you see a road being laid or repaired by the municipality in your locality or reviving of a lake that waters acreage, think about the cost involved and compare it with the possible taxes people in your community pay, including yourself. If the taxes the community pay, you think, do not make up to this single expenditure, think about all the projects undertaken, border protection and people employed in the government. True, there are indirect taxes also such as the GST that replaced about 700 distinct types of taxes in India until 2016. But the majority of India's revenues do not come from individual tax payers. In 2017, personal income tax accounted for only 2% of India's GDP. Again, that is no reason to consider individual income tax insignificant and non-contributing. A sensible and responsible citizen draws a line between proper use of the taxes and the responsibility towards his country. But, that aside, let us look at some aspects of tax that concern individual assessees or tax payers.

Understanding the rules

[Income tax is a tax levied by the Government of India on the income of every person. The provisions governing the Income-tax are covered in the Income-tax Act, 1961. It is levied on the annual income of a person. The year under the Income-tax Law is the period starting from 1st April and ending on 31st March of next calendar year. The Income-tax Law classifies the year as (1) Previous year, and (2) Assessment year. The year in which income is earned is called as previous year and the year in which the income is charged to tax is called as assessment year e.g. income earned during the period of 1st April 2018 to 31st March 2019 is treated as income of the previous year 2018-19. Income of the previous year 2018-19 will be charged to tax in the next year i.e. in the assessment year 2019-20. For filing the return, you can take the help of tax professionals or the help of Public Relations Officer [PRO] in the local office of the Income-tax Department. You may also take assistance from Tax Return Preparers [TRPs]. Under the Income-tax Act, every person has the responsibility to correctly compute and pay his due taxes. Where the Department finds that there has been understatement of income and resultant tax due, it takes measures to compute the actual tax amount that ought to have been paid. This demand raised on the person is called as Tax on regular assessment.

The NSDL website provides online services called as Challan Status Enquiry. You can also check your tax credit by viewing your Form 26AS from your e-filing account at www.incometaxindiaefiling.gov.in. Form 26AS will also disclose the credit of TDS/TCS in your account. Once taxes are paid, you are responsible for ensuring that the tax credits are available in your tax credit statement and TDS/TCS certificates received by you and that full particulars of income and tax payment are submitted to the Income-tax Department in the form of Return of Income which is to be filed before the due date prescribed in this regard. For every source of income, you must maintain proof of earning and the records specified under the Income-tax Act. In case no such records are prescribed, you should maintain reasonable records with which you can support the claim of income.

Income tax rules mandate that every individual who has a gross total income (before applying any deduction benefits) exceeding the basic exemption limit must file the 'Return' of income every year. Such total income shall include the income of any other person in respect of whom the individual is assessable. Though the return filing process is made online (unlike the conventional method of submitting returns on paper), diverse types of forms are used for filing returns for different incomes and sources. There are five heads of income defined under the Act viz. income from – Salary, House Property, Capital Gains, Business / Profession and Other Sources. The most commonly used form by individuals having income from salary, house property and other sources is 'ITR1 (SAHAJ)'. If the assessee makes any mistake in the return filed, the same can be revised and resubmitted before the end of the relevant assessment year. Sometimes, it happens so that the income of a person is subjected to 'Tax Deduction at Source' (TDS) at the rates specified by the Act. If the employer or the person making the payment is required by law to deduct such amount irrespective of the tax liability of the receiver, the assessee, through the return can claim a refund of such tax deduction, if he is eligible for it.

PAN: As per the Income Tax Act, 1961, a 'Person' is defined to include (i) an individual, (ii) a Hindu undivided family, (iii) a company, (iv) a firm, (v) an association of persons or a body of individuals, whether incorporated or not, (vi) a local authority, and (vii) every artificial juridical person, not falling within any of the preceding sub-clauses. However, as this section is concerned with individuals, the term person implies an individual. As per the rules, every person who has a total income in a fiscal year exceeding the specified basic tax exemption limit, must apply for and obtain a Permanent Account Number (PAN), a ten-character code in the combination of alphabets and numbers. However, regardless of the total income, even to carryout certain financial transactions, sometimes above a certain limit, one must have a valid PAN. Such limits or transactions can be purchasing a vehicle, making bank-deposits, opening demat (common term for dematerialisation) accounts, investing in mutual funds, paying life insurance premium etc. Under no circumstances whatever, a person cannot and must not hold more than one PAN.]

KYC: For making any financial transaction mostly in the banking, financial services, and insurance industry, subsequent to PAN, there is another regulatory requirement known as Know Your Customer (KYC). *KYC is a one-time exercise while dealing in securities markets. Once KYC is done through a SEBI registered intermediary (broker, depository participant, mutual fund etc.), one need not undergo the same process again when they approach another intermediary. In case of any change in KYC details, one need to submit a change request form along with the supporting documents. The provisions of The Prevention of Money Laundering Act, 2002 (PMLA) and KRA Regulations (2011) make it mandatory for all market participants to comply with the KYC norms. As a result, all persons will now have to submit their PAN card copy (which serves as Proof of Identity (PoI)) and Proof of Address (PoA) only once with any of the intermediary they deal with.* Only after successfully getting the KYC registered can a person open accounts such as demat and transact in share, mutual funds etc. Of course, practically, KYC forms can be submitted along with various account opening forms or investment and transaction forms that will be processed by intermediaries simultaneously.

<u>Aadhaar</u>: For an Indian, Aadhaar requires no introduction. It is like a social security number that is different from the tax identification number – PAN. *Aadhaar number is a 12-digit random number issued by the Unique Identification Authority of India (UIDAI) to the residents of India after satisfying the verification process laid down by it. Any individual, irrespective of age and gender, who is a resident of India, may voluntarily enrol to obtain Aadhaar number. A person willing to enrol for Aadhaar must provide minimal demographic and biometric information during the enrolment process. An individual need to enrol for Aadhaar only once and after de-duplication, only one Aadhaar shall be generated, as the uniqueness is achieved through the process of demographic and biometric de-duplication. Aadhaar is a strategic policy tool for social and financial inclusion, public sector delivery reforms, managing fiscal budgets, increase convenience and promote hassle-free people-centric governance. Aadhaar can be used as a permanent Financial Address and facilitates financial inclusion of the underprivileged and weaker sections of the society and is therefore a tool of distributive justice and equality. Linking of Aadhaar with PAN is mandatory now, which must be completed before the end of the financial year 2018-19 by the PAN holders requiring filing of Income Tax Return. Constitutional validity of Aadhaar has been upheld by the Hon'ble Supreme Court of India in September 2018. Consequently, in terms of Section 139AA of Income Tax Act, 1961 and order dated 30.6.2018 of the Central Board of Direct Taxes, Aadhaar-PAN linking is mandatory now which must be completed till 31.3.2019 by the PAN holders requiring filing of Income Tax Return.*

Concerning individuals

<u>Minor</u>: Experts say that one must not hold sentimental value to their investments. Without an insisting adviser, investors tend to hold on to some scrips despite their inferior performance, like the tolerance humans show towards a spoilt and troublesome child. In India, sentiments go beyond investments. More than making an investment that can deliver impressive return, some people are keen about investing in the names of their minor children, something that I seriously discourage and dislike. Investment in the name of a minor can be done by providing details of the Guardian (parents are considered as natural and legal guardians), even though the minor in whose name investment is being done does not hold a valid PAN or KYC or a Bank account. Merely the name on the investment application is that of the minor and all other details belong to the guardian. Does that mean minors can manage the investment? No. It is the adults/guardians that manage it. Just as they started the investment, they can redeem it. It is only that they feel if the investment is in the name of the minor child, they hold sentimental value to it and resist from withdrawing. But in my experience, that has never been a barrier for parents for redeeming the investments in the name of minors. I believe that if one genuinely loves their children, care for them and their future, they need not deceive themselves and make investments in the names of minors. They can directly make investments in their own name and simply assign it (mentally or through a financial plan in writing) to the children's goals. Besides, minor investments only increase the paper work. After they attain the age of majority, the investments will have to be shifted to the names of grown up children but after they obtain a

PAN and get their KYC registered. Certain investments may have restrictions in the cases of minors that complicate the process and often leading to frequent transaction failures. I personally feel that financial product manufacturers give the option of investing in a minor's name only to take advantage of the sentiments of Indian investors. I do not see any other purpose for it. Nonetheless, it is up to the reader, investor, and adviser to decide in this matter.

<u>Senior Citizen</u>: As per the prevailing tax laws, an individual who is of the age of 60 years or above but less than 80 year at any time during the respective year is considered as a senior citizen. Individuals who are of the age of 80 or above at any time during the respective year are considered as very senior citizens. Senior citizens and very senior citizens are granted a higher exemption limit as compared to normal tax payers. Exemption limit is the quantum of income up to which a person is not liable to pay tax. The tax benefits offered under the Income-tax Law to a senior citizen or a very senior citizen are available only to resident senior citizen and resident very senior citizens. In other words, these benefits are not available to a non-resident, even though he or she may be of higher age. From the assessment year 2018-19 onwards, any taxpayer filing return of income in Form ITR1 or ITR4 and having a refund claim in the return or having total income that is more than the specified limit is required to furnish the return of income electronically with or without digital signature or by using electronic verification code. However, Income-tax Law grants relaxation from e-filing in above case to very senior citizens. Similarly, interest income from deposits with banks or post office or co-operative banks earned by senior citizens up to the specified limit are eligible

for deduction. Further, currently no tax is deducted at source on interest income up to the limits specified under the law.

Clubbing of Income: Normally, a person is taxed in respect of income earned by him only. However, in certain cases income of other person is included (clubbed) in the taxable income of the taxpayer and in such a case he will be liable to pay tax in respect of his income if any, as well as income of other person too. The situation in which income of other person is included in the income of the taxpayer is called as clubbing of income e.g. income of minor child is clubbed with the income of his/her parent. if a person transfers income from an asset owned by him without transferring the asset from which the income is generated, then the income from such an asset is taxed in the hands of the transferor i.e. person transferring the income. Income of minor child earned on account of manual work or any activity involving application of his/her skill, knowledge, talent, experience, etc. will not be clubbed with the income of his/her parent. However, accretion from such income will be clubbed with the income of parent of such minor. Income of minor will be clubbed with the income of that parent whose income (excluding minor's income) is higher. For example, Mr. Raj has given a bungalow owned by him on rent. Annual rent of the bungalow is Rs. 84000. He transferred entire rental income to his friend Mr. Kumar. However, he did not transfer the bungalow. In this situation, rent of Rs. 84000 will be taxed in the hands of Mr. Raj. If an individual transfer (directly or indirectly) his/her asset to his or her spouse otherwise than for adequate consideration, then income from such asset will be clubbed with the income of the individual i.e. transferor. Under certain circumstances, remuneration i.e. salary received by the spouse of an individual from a concern in which the individual is having substantial interest is clubbed with the income of the individual. An individual shall be deemed to have substantial interest in any concern, if such individual alone or along with his relatives beneficially holds at any time during the previous year 20% or more of the equity shares (in case of a company) or is entitled to 20% of profit (in case of concern other than a company). Relative for this purpose includes husband, wife, brother or sister or lineal ascendant or descendent of that individual. In case the reader has any queries relating to clubbing of incomes, I advise consulting a Chartered Accountant or a practising tax professional.

Income from Salary: [As per the Act, Salary (one of the five heads of income) is defined to include a) Wages b) Annuity c) Pension d) Gratuity e) Fees, Commission, Perquisites, Profits in lieu of or in addition to Salary or Wages f) Advance of Salary g) Leave Encashment h) Annual accretion to the balance of Recognized Provident Fund i) Transferred balance in Recognized Provident Fund and j) Contribution by Central Government or any other employer to Employees Pension Account as referred in Sec. 80CCD. Salary income is chargeable to tax on "due basis" or "receipt basis" whichever is earlier. Existence of relationship of employer and employee is must between the payer and payee to tax the income under this head. Income from salary taxable during the year consists of salary due from employer (including former employer) to taxpayer during the previous year whether paid or not, salary paid by employer (including former employer) to taxpayer during the previous year before it became due, and arrear of salary paid by the employer (including former employer) to taxpayer during the previous year, if not charged to tax in any earlier year. As an exception, remuneration, bonus, or commission received by a partner from the firm is not taxable under the head Salaries. It would be taxable under the head business or profession. The place of accrual of salary depends on the place where the services are rendered even if it is paid outside India. Salary paid by the Foreign Government to his employee serving in India is taxable under the head Salaries. Leave salary paid abroad in respect of leave earned in India shall be deemed to accrue or arise in India. However, if a Citizen of India renders services outside India, and receives salary from Government of India, it would be taxable as salary deemed to have accrued in India. Basic salary, dearness allowance, bonus, fees, and commission are fully taxable. We shall see some important deduction and exemption benefits in the next section.]

Income from House Property: [It shall be taxable under this head if three conditions are satisfied viz. a) The house property should consist of any building or land appurtenant thereto; b) The taxpayer should be the owner of the property; c) The house property should not be used for the purpose of business or profession carried on by the taxpayer.

Particulars	Amount
Gross Annual Value	-
Less: Municipal Taxes	-
Net Annual Value	xxxx
Less: Standard Deduction @ 30%	-
Less: Interest on borrowed capital	-
Income from House Property	xxxx

The Gross Annual Value of the house property shall be higher of a) Expected rent, i.e. the sum for which the property might be expected to be let out from year to year. Expected rent shall be higher of municipal valuation or fair rent of the property, subject to maximum of standard rent; b) Rent received or receivable after excluding unrealized rent but before deducting loss due to vacancy. Out of sum thus computed, any loss incurred due to vacancy in the house property shall be deducted and the remaining sum so computed shall be deemed to the gross annual value. Municipal taxes including service-taxes levied by any local authority in respect of house property is allowed as deduction, if a) Taxes are borne by the owner; and b) Taxes are actually paid by him during the year.

30% of net annual value of the house property is allowed as deduction if property is let-out during the previous year.

<u>Income from Other Sources</u>: This is the residual head of income. Hence, any income which is not specifically taxed under any other head of income will be taxed under this head. Further, there are certain incomes which are always taxed under this head. Some of these incomes are certain dividends; winnings from lotteries, crossword puzzles, races including horse races, card game and other game of any sort, gambling, or betting of any form whatsoever; interest received on compensation or on enhanced compensation; gifts etc. One should refer the prevailing laws or seek advice of a professional tax consultant or a chartered accountant rather than making assumptions or being uncertain or depending on redundant information.]

Making the best out of benefits

Between us, we know that paying taxes is our duty as a responsible citizen. But it also feels that if we want to know what is taxable, we just have to think, taxing of what causes us discomfort and, in that lie, all the tax rules. But tax law is not cruel and all taxing. Besides, for reasons whatever, the Government does not work for itself. Its existence is for its people. So, it does not tax its citizens unreasonably. There are also some provisions in the Act that have been introduced for the welfare of the tax payers, some for low income earners to reduce the tax burden and some to encourage public to take sensible financial decisions for their better financial future. These provisions also labelled as tax benefits are mentioned in the Act under various sections as Exemption and Deduction. One should understand the difference between the two terms to make the best use of the provisions laid down in the Act, besides avoiding confusion while doing the assessment and filing the returns. An exemption is applied during the process of calculating gross total income and is equally available to all tax payers, whoever has the specified exempted income. If an income is exempted, it is not chargeable to tax and removed before arriving at total income. Conversely, a deduction is applied after calculating total income, depending on certain conditions. If you are wondering what difference it makes whether you remove it before calculating total income or after calculating it, understand that it is not merely about subtracting but the nature of exemption applicable to all those, earning exempted income and the amount of deduction applicable to all those that have taken necessary actions. To make it simpler, exemption is for inflows (income) and deduction is on account of outflows. Additionally, there is a rebate for individuals. [Tax rebate in case of individual resident in India, whose total income does not exceed Rs. 3.50 Lakhs shall be allowed a rebate in income tax for an amount equal to hundred per cent of such income-tax or an amount of Rs. 2500, whichever is less.

Deduction and Exemption

Deduction: These benefits under Chapter VIA of the IT Act have been specified from Sections 80C to 80U and a few other sections. Note that the sections or benefits may be changed or scrapped by the government anytime.

With effect from 2019-20, under **Sec 16(ia)**, there shall be a standard deduction of Rs. 40000 applicable to salaried individuals, which is deductible from gross salary. Two other allowances viz. medical reimbursement to the extent of Rs. 15000 and transport allowance up to Rs. 19200 have been removed to make way for this single larger benefit. In comparison to the existing benefits that have been replaced, it is a mere extra of Rs. 5800, on which those that fall into the current 5% tax slab will save extra tax of just Rs. 290, of course before applying any deduction or loading cess. Nevertheless, such small savings aggregate to big volumes and one must keep an open mind and appreciate that medical exemption is not limited to Rs. 15000.

Life insurance premium paid towards a policy on the life of assessee, assessee's spouse and any child; contributions made by an employee to the Employees' Provident Fund; approved Superannuation Fund; contribution (investment) made by an individual to Public Provident Fund and/or Sukanya Samriddhi Yojana, National Savings Certificate, Equity Linked Savings Schemes of mutual funds, Senior Citizen Savings Scheme, and Five-year bank or post-office fixed deposit; Tuition fees paid towards full-time education of any two children; principal component of instalments paid toward housing loan (after construction is complete) under **Sec 80C** – are all eligible for a collective deduction of up to Rs. 1.50 Lakh in a fiscal year. With effect from assessment year 2016-17 a new sub-section (1B) under 80CCD is inserted to provide for additional deduction to the extent of Rs. 50000 for investments made in approved pension plans such as the National Pension System (NPS). Contribution to NPS is enjoys additional deduction and is not subject to ceiling limit of Rs. 1.50 Lakh. Aggregate amount of deduction in any case shall not exceed Rs. 1 Lakh in an assessment year.

Some other deduction benefits include – Interest on deposits in savings bank accounts up to Rs. 10000 per year under **80TTA**; interest up to Rs. 50000 per year on deposit in saving account or fixed deposit specifically made by a senior citizen under **80TTB**; deduction to a resident individual who, at any time during the previous year, is certified by the medical authority to be a person with disability up to Rs. 75000 and in the case of a person with severe disability, Rs. 1.25 Lakh under **Sec 80U**; donations to notified associations or funds such as the National Defence Fund, Prime Minister's National Relief Fund, National Children's Fund, Government or approved association for promoting family planning, universities and approved educational institutions of national eminence, National Foundation for Communal Harmony, Army Central Welfare Fund, Indian Naval Benevolent Fund and Air Force Central Welfare Fund, National Illness Assistance Fund, National Sports Fund, National Cultural Fund, Fund for Technology Development and Application, Indian Olympic Association, etc. are eligible for 100% deduction benefit while Donations to certain approved funds, trusts, charitable institutions/ donations for renovation or repairs of notified temples, etc. are deductible up to 50% under **Sec 80G**.

<u>Note on Sec 80D</u>: As per section 80D, an individual can claim deduction in respect of the following payments.

1. Medical insurance premium paid by assessee, being individual by any mode other than cash.
2. Any contribution made by assessee, being individual to Central Government Health Scheme or such other Scheme as may be notified by the Central Government
3. Sum paid by assessee, being individual on account of preventive health check-up
4. Medical expenditure incurred by assessee, being individual on the health of a senior citizen person provided that no amount has been paid to effect or to keep in force an insurance on the health of such person

In case of an individual, deduction is available in respect of medical insurance policy taken in his own name, or in the name his/her spouse, his/her parents, and his/her dependent children. Deduction on account of medical expenditure shall be allowed only when it is incurred on the health of the aforementioned persons who are senior citizens. 'Senior citizen' means an individual resident in India who is of the age of sixty years or more at any time during the relevant previous year. In case of an individual, amount of deduction cannot exceed the following.

1. Rs. 25000, in aggregate, in respect of medical insurance premium or any payment made for preventive health check-up. This deduction is available if payment is made for benefit of assessee, himself or his/her spouse or dependent children.
2. Rs. 25000, in aggregate, in respect of medical insurance premium or any payment made for preventive health check-up. This deduction is available if payment is made for benefit of parents of assessee.
3. Rs 25000 in aggregate in respect of contribution made to the Central Government Health Scheme or any scheme notified by the Central Government This deduction is available if payment is made for benefit of assessee, himself, his/her spouse, or dependent children.
4. Rs 50000 in aggregate in respect of medical expenditure incurred on the health of assessee, himself, his/her spouse or dependent children or parents. This deduction is available if amount is paid for benefit of a senior citizen and no amount has been paid to effect or to keep in force an insurance on the health of such person.

Total amount of deduction for the expenditure incurred on preventive health check-up of assessee, his family and parents could not exceed Rs. 5000. In aforesaid clauses of a, b and c, additional deduction of Rs 25000 is available when medical insurance is taken on the life of senior citizen.

Disability includes blindness, low vision, leprosy-cured, hearing impairment, locomotor's disability, mental retardation and mental illness, autism, cerebral palsy, multiple disability. Person with severe disability means a person with 80% or more of one or more disabilities, as referred to in section 56(4) of the Persons with Disabilities (Equal Opportunities, Protection of Rights and Full Participation) Act, 1995 (1 of 1996); or a person with severe disability referred to in clause (o) of section 2 of the National Trust for Welfare of Persons with Autism, Cerebral Palsy, Mental Retardation and Multiple Disabilities Act, 1999 (44 of 1999). A resident individual, incurring expenditure on maintenance of relative dependent, being a person with disability, can claim deduction under section 80DD. Deduction is available in respect of the expenditure incurred on medical treatment (including nursing), training, rehabilitation of a dependent person with disability and amount paid or deposited under a scheme of LIC or any other insurer or UTI or specified company duly approved by the Board, for maintenance of dependent person with disability. Dependent person with disability includes spouse, children, parents, brothers, and sisters of the individual, or any of them who is mainly or wholly dependent on such individual provided that such dependent person has not claimed any deduction under section 80U.

If the taxpayer incurs any expenditure as mentioned in (a) or (b) above, then a flat deduction of Rs. 75000 is available, irrespective of the amount of such expenditure. However, if the dependent person is suffering from severe disability i.e. disability of 80% or above, then the amount of deduction will be Rs. 125000. While claiming deduction under section 80DD, the taxpayer should obtain a copy of certificate issued by the medical authority. If the dependent predeceases the taxpayer, then amount paid or deposited in (b) above, shall be charged to tax in the hands of the taxpayer for the previous year in which such sum is received.

As per section 80DDB, a taxpayer can claim deduction in respect of expenditure incurred by him on medical treatment of specified diseases. The provisions in this regard are as follows: [As amended by Finance Act, 2018] 1) Deduction under section 80DDB can be claimed by an individual, who is resident in India. 2) Deduction is available in respect of amount actually paid by the taxpayer on medical treatment of specified disease or ailment (prescribed by the Board, see rule 11DD for prescribed disease or ailment). 3) In case of an individual, the previously mentioned expenditure should be incurred on medical treatment of an individual or wholly/mainly dependent spouse, children, parents, brothers, and sisters of the individual. The tax payer must obtain the prescription for the medical treatment from a neurologist, an oncologist, a urologist, a haematologist, an immunologist, or such other specialist, as may be prescribed. Amount of deduction will be lower of the following: (a) amount actually paid on medical treatment specified above; or (b) Rs. 40000. However, the limit of Rs. 40000 will be increased to Rs. 1 Lakh, if the expenditure is incurred on medical treatment of a senior citizen i.e. any resident individual of age of 60 years or above.

Exemption: An exempt income is not charged to tax, i.e., Income-tax Law specifically grants exemption from tax to such income. Incomes which are chargeable to tax are called taxable incomes. Unlike most deductions, exemption is applied to different heads of incomes, separately.

Agricultural Income

As per section 10(1), agricultural income earned by the taxpayer in India is exempt from tax. As per section 2(1A), agricultural income generally means (a) any rent or revenue derived from land which is situated in India and is used for agricultural purposes (b) any income derived from such land by agriculture operations including processing of agricultural produce so as to render it fit for the market or sale of such produce (c) any income attributable to a farm house subject to satisfaction of certain conditions specified in this regard in section 2(1A). Any income derived from saplings or seedlings grown in a nursery shall be deemed to be agricultural income.

Gratuity

Gratuity received by Government Employees (Other than employees of statutory corporations) is fully exempt from tax. In the case of Death-cum-Retirement Gratuity received by other employees who are covered under Gratuity Act, 1972 (other than Government employee), least of following amounts is exempt from tax:

1. (*15/26) X Last drawn salary** X completed years of service
2. Rs. 20,00,000 (Rupees Twenty Lakhs – current provision)
3. Gratuity actually received.

*7 days in case of employee of seasonal establishment

** Salary = Last drawn salary including DA but excluding any bonus, commission, HRA, overtime and any other allowance, benefits, or perquisite

In the case of Death-cum-Retirement Gratuity received by other employees who are covered under Gratuity Act, 1972 (other than Government employee), least of following amounts is exempt from tax:

1. Half month's Average Salary* X Completed years of service
2. Rs. 10,00,000 (Rupees Ten Lakhs)
3. Gratuity actually received.

*Average salary = Average Salary of last 10 months immediately preceding the month of retirement

** Salary = Basic Pay + DA (to the extent it forms part of retirement benefits) + turnover based commission

Housing Loan Interest

In respect of self-occupied residential house property, interest incurred on capital borrowed for the purpose of acquisition or construction of house property shall be allowed as deduction up to Rs. 2 lakhs. The deduction shall be allowed if acquisition or construction of house property is completed within 5 years. If the acquisition or construction of the property is not completed within 5 years from the end of the year in which loan was taken, interest shall be allowed as deduction up to Rs. 30000 only. Any interest pertaining to the period prior to the year of acquisition/construction of the house property shall be allowed as deduction in five equal instalments, beginning with the year in which the property was acquired/constructed. The amounts of deduction benefits specified may shift in either direction in the future. In respect of interest on borrowed capital on let-out property, actual interest incurred on capital borrowed for the purpose of acquisition, construction, repairing, re-construction shall be allowed as deduction.

Long Term Capital Gain

Long-term capital gains arising from land or building, or both, invested in long-term specified asset issued by institutions such as the Rural Electrification Corporation Limited or National Highways Authority of India are exempt from tax up to a maximum investment Rs. 50 lakhs in a fiscal year, under Sec 54(EC). For example, if the property was bought in 2003-04 for Rs. 5 Lakhs and sold in 2018-19, the indexed cost of acquisition is 500000 x (280/105) = 13.33 Lakhs. Suppose the property is sold for Rs. 60 Lakhs in 2018-19. The long-term capital gains calculate to Rs. 60 Lakhs – 13.33 Lakhs = 46.66 Lakhs, on which 20% (after indexation) must be paid as tax. The tax thus computed come to Rs. 9.33 Lakhs. This amount may be invested in the notified capital gains bonds under Sec 54(EC) within six months from the sale of the property or invested in another property (within two years for purchase or three years for construction). While the bonds currently have a lock-in period of 5 years, the property bought for saving tax must not be sold within 5 years. Long-term capital gains in case of equity i.e. gains made on sale after a holding period of 12 months were fully exempt from tax earlier. However, currently they have been made taxable with some conditions. If the long-term gain on sale of equity in any fiscal year is less than Rs. 1 Lakh, the gain is fully exempt from tax. However, if the gain is more than Rs. 1 Lakh, only the excess amount (excluding the initial 1 Lakh) is taxable at a flat rate of 10%.

Agricultural Land: Say, a farmer wants to shift his agricultural land for certain reason and hence he sold his old agricultural land and from the sale proceeds he purchased another agricultural land. In this case the objective of the seller was not to earn income by sale of old land but was to shift to another land. If in this case, the seller was liable to pay income-tax on capital gains arising on sale of old land, then it would be a hardship on him. Section 54B gives relief from such a hardship. Section 54B gives relief to a taxpayer who sells his agricultural land and from the sale proceeds he acquires another agricultural land. For this exemption, the asset transferred should be agricultural land. The land may be a long-term capital asset or short-term capital asset. The agricultural land should be used by the individual or his parents for agricultural purpose at least for a period of two years immediately preceding the date of transfer. Within a period of two years from the date of transfer of old land, the taxpayer should acquire another agricultural land. The amount of exemption under section 54B will be lower of the amount of – capital gains arising on transfer of agricultural land or the investment in new agricultural land including the amount deposited in Capital Gains Deposit Account Scheme. Exemption under section 54B is available in respect of rollover of capital gains arising on transfer of agricultural land into another agricultural land. However, to keep a check on misutilisation of this benefit a restriction is inserted in section 54B. The restriction is in the form of prohibition of sale of the new agricultural land. If a taxpayer purchases new agricultural land to claim exemption under section 54B and subsequently he transfers the new agricultural land within a period of 3 years from the date of its acquisition, then the benefit granted under section 54B will be withdrawn. The ultimate impact of the restriction is a) the restriction will be attracted if, after claiming exemption under section 54B, the new agricultural land is sold within a period of 3 years from the date of its purchase; b) if the agricultural land is sold within a period of 3 years from the date of its purchase, then at the time of computation of capital gain arising on transfer of the new land, the amount of capital gain claimed as exemption under section 54B will be deducted from the cost of acquisition of the new agricultural land.

Computation of capital gains for the year 2019-20	
Particulars	Rs.
Full sale value of new agricultural land	xxxxx
Less: Expenditure incurred on transfer of land	xxx
Net sale consideration	xxxxx
Less: Cost of acquisition	xxx
Short- term capital gains on sale of new agricultural land	xxxx

Computation of cost of acquisition	
Particulars	Rs.
Cost of acquisition of new land	xxxxx
Less: Exemption claimed earlier under section 54B	xxxx
Cost of new land to be used while computing capital gain	xxxxx

To claim exemption under section 54B, the taxpayer should purchase another agricultural land within a period of two years from the date of transfer of old land. If till the date of filing the return of income the capital gain arising on transfer of the old land is not utilised (in whole or in part) for purchase of another agricultural land, then the benefit of exemption can be availed by depositing the unutilised amount in Capital Gains Deposit Account Scheme in any branch of public sector bank. The new land can be purchased by withdrawing the amount from the said account within the specified time-limit of 2 years.

Leave Travel Concession

An employee can claim exemption under section 10(5) in respect of Leave Travel Concession. Exemption under section 10(5) is available to all employees (i.e. Indian as well as foreign citizens). Exemption is available in respect of value of any travel concession or assistance received or due to the employee from his employer (including former employer) for himself and his family members in connection with his proceeding on leave to any place in India. Other provisions to be kept in mind in this regard are as follows: Where journey is performed by air: Amount of exemption will be lower of amount of economy class air fare of the National Carrier by the shortest route or actual amount spent. Where journey is performed by rail: Amount of exemption will be lower of amount of airconditioned first class rail fare by the shortest route or actual amount spent. The same rule will apply where journey is performed by any other mode and the place of origin of journey and destination are connected by rail. Where the place of origin and destination are not connected by rail and journey is performed by any mode of transport other than by air: The exemption will be as follows: (a) If recognised public transport exists: Exemption will be lower of first class or deluxe class fare by the shortest route or actual amount spent. (b) If no recognised public transport exists: Exemption will be lower of amount of airconditioned first class rail fare by the shortest route (considering as if journey is performed by rail) or actual amount spent. Block: Exemption is available for 2 journeys in a block of 4 years. The block applicable for current period is calendar year 2014-17. The previous block was of calendar year 2010-2013. Carry over: If an employee has not availed of travel concession or assistance in respect of one or two permitted journeys in a block of 4 years, then he is entitled to carry over one journey to the next block. In this situation, exemption will be available for 3 journeys in the next block. However, to avail of this benefit, exemption in respect of journey should be utilised in the first calendar year of the next block. In other words, in case of carry over, exemption is available in respect of 3 journeys in a block, provided exemption in respect of at least 1 journey is claimed in the first year of the next block. Exemption is in respect of actual expenditure on fare, hence, if no journey is performed, then no exemption is available. Family: Family will include spouse and children of the individual, whether dependent or not and parents, brothers, sisters of the individual or any of them who are wholly or mainly dependent on him.

House Rent Allowance

The amount which is not to be included in the total income of an assessee in respect of the special allowance referred to in clause (13A) of section 10 shall be the least of the three – (a) the actual amount of such allowance received by the assessee in respect of the relevant period; or (b) the amount by which the expenditure actually incurred by the assessee in payment of rent in respect of residential accommodation occupied by him exceeds one-tenth of the amount of salary due to the assessee in respect of the relevant period; or (c) an amount equal to (i) one-half of the amount of salary due to the assessee in respect of the relevant period where such accommodation is situate at Bombay, Calcutta, Delhi or Madras; and (ii) two-fifth of the amount of salary due to the assessee in respect of the relevant period where such accommodation is situated at any other place. To put it simpler, least of the following is exempt from tax.

1. Actual HRA Received
2. 40% of Salary (50%, if house situated in Mumbai, Calcutta, Delhi, or Chennai)
3. Rent paid minus 10% of salary

Salary = Basic + DA (if part of retirement benefit) + Turnover based Commission

HRA is fully taxable, if it is received by an employee who is living in his own house or if he does not pay any rent. It is mandatory for employee to report PAN of the property owner to the employer if rent paid is more than Rs. 1 Lakh.

Minor's Income

In case the income of individual includes income of a minor child, such individual can claim an exemption under section 10(32)) of Rs. 1500 or income of minor so clubbed, whichever is less. Provisions of section 64(1A) will not apply to any income of a minor child suffering from disability specified under section 80U. In other words, income of a minor suffering from disability specified under section 80U will not be clubbed with the income of his/her parent.

There are a ton of other allowances provided under the Income Tax Act. Mentioning them all will make this a book on taxation. One must refer the law and latest amendments and rules or consult a chartered accountant or a tax consultant for more information.

Miscellaneous Taxes

Gift Tax: A quite common and frequent question running in the mind of taxpayers is the taxability of gifts. In this part, you can gain knowledge about various provisions relating to taxability of gift received by an individual i.e. sum of money or property received by an individual without consideration or a case in which the property is acquired for inadequate consideration. From the taxation point of view, gift can be classified as monetary gift, gift of movable property and gift of immovable property. Sum of money received without consideration i.e. monetary gift received in cash, cheque, draft, etc. by an individual is chargeable to tax if the aggregate value of such sum received during the year exceeds Rs. 50000. The key point to be noted in this regard is the "aggregate value of such sum received during the year". The taxability of the gift is determined based on the aggregate value of gift received during the year and not based on individual gift. Hence, if the aggregate value of gifts received during the year exceeds Rs. 50000, then total value of all such gifts received during the year will be charged to tax i.e. the total amount of gift and not the amount in excess of Rs. 50000. Gift received on the occasion of wedding of the individual is not charged to tax. Apart from marriage there is no other occasion when monetary gift received by an individual is not charged to tax. Hence, monetary gift received on occasions like birthday, anniversary, etc. will be charged to tax. Gifts received from relatives are not charged to tax. Relative for this purpose means a) spouse of the individual; b) brother or sister of the individual; c) brother or sister of the spouse of the individual; d) brother or sister of either of the parents of the individual; e) any lineal ascendant or descendent of the individual; f) any lineal ascendant or descendent of the spouse of the individual; g) spouses of the persons referred to from (b) to (f). Friend is not a 'relative' as defined in the above list and hence, gift received from friends will be charged to tax. Taxable value of gifts is chargeable under the head 'Income from Other Sources'.

Capital Gains: The taxability of capital gains depends on the nature of gain, i.e., whether short-term or long-term. Hence, to determine the taxability, capital gains are to be classified into short-term and long-term. In other words, the tax rates for long-term capital gain and short-term capital gain are different. With effect from the F.Y. 2017-18, in case of property, it is treated as long term if it is held for at least 24 months (previously 36 months). In exemptions, we saw that investment of long-term capital gains from property if invested in notified bonds are exempt up to Rs. 50 Lakhs. But what if the gain exceeds the limit or you are not willing to invest in the bonds for several reasons? You are required to pay tax at 20% with indexation. Indexation means, inflating the cost of acquisition of property to the present day (due to inflation) based on the Cost Inflation Index (CII). The CII Index has been revised with base year as 2001-02, starting at 100. The table up to the current year is below. In case of debt, the period to determine whether the gain is short-term or long-term in nature is taken as 36 months and the taxation is similar to that of property i.e. 20% with indexation benefit. Refer the example given in the previous section under Exemption.

Cost Inflation Index – CII					
Year	Index	Year	Index	Year	Index
2001-02	100	2007-08	129	2013-14	220
2002-03	105	2008-09	137	2014-15	240
2003-04	109	2009-10	148	2015-16	254
2004-05	113	2010-11	167	2016-17	264
2005-06	117	2011-12	184	2017-18	272
2006-07	122	2012-13	200	2018-19	280

Indexed cost of acquisition = Actual cost of acquisition x (Current year index/Base year index)

To sum up, period for determining long-term is 12 months for equity, 24 months for property and 36 months for debt, gold, and others. Likewise, LTCG tax in case of equity is exempted up to Rs. 1 Lakh per annum, up to Rs. 50 Lakhs in case of property if invested in bonds, and fully taxable as per rules in case of debt and others.

Short-term capital gain arising on account of transfer of short-term capital asset is computed as follows:

Particulars	Rs.
Full value of consideration (i.e. Sales value of the asset)	xxxxx
Less: Expenditure incurred in connection with transfer of capital asset	(xxxxx)
Net Sale Consideration	xxxxx

Less: Cost of acquisition (i.e. the purchase price of the capital asset)	(xxxxx)
Less: Cost of improvement (i.e. post purchases capital expenses on improvement)	(xxxxx)
Short-Term Capital Gains	xxxxx

For the purpose of determination of tax rate, short-term capital gains are classified as Short-term capital gains covered under section 111A and Short-term capital gains other than covered under section 111A. Examples of STCG covered under section 111A are STCG arising on sale of equity shares listed in a recognised stock exchange or units of equity oriented mutual fund which are chargeable to STT. Examples of STCG not covered under section 111A are STCG arising on sale of equity shares other than through a recognised stock exchange, STCG arising on sale of shares other than equity shares, STCG arising on sale of units of non-equity oriented mutual fund (debt oriented mutual funds) STCG on debentures, bonds and Government securities, STCG on sale of assets other than shares/units like STCG on sale of immovable property, gold, silver, etc. STCG covered under section 111A is charged to tax @ 15% (plus surcharge and cess as applicable) Normal STCG, i.e., STCG other than covered under section 111A is charged to tax at normal rate of tax which is determined based on the total taxable income of the taxpayer.

Asset	LTCG		STCG	
	Period	Rate	Period	Rate
Equity	>= 12 Months	Nil < 1 Lakh	< 12 Months	15% Flat
Property	>= 24 Months	20% with Indexation	< 24 Months	As per slab
Debt	>= 36 Months	20% with Indexation	< 36 Months	As per slab

Only a resident individual and resident HUF can adjust the exemption limit against STCG covered under section 111A. Thus, a non-resident individual/HUF cannot adjust the exemption limit against STCG covered under section 111A. A resident individual/HUF can adjust the STCG covered under section 111A against the basic exemption limit, but such adjustment is possible only after making adjustment of other income. In other words, first income other than STCG covered under section 111A is to be adjusted against the exemption limit and then the remaining limit (if any) can be adjusted against STCG covered under section 111A.

<u>Income from other sources</u>: Besides, gifts, there are some other incomes that are taxable under this head. It is the residual head of income. Hence, any income which is not specifically taxed under any other head of income will be taxed under this. Further, there are certain incomes which are always taxed under this head. These incomes are as follows:

1. As per section 56(2)(i), dividends are always taxed under this head. However, dividends from domestic company other than those covered by section 2(22)(e) are exempt from tax under section 10(34).
2. Winnings from lotteries, crossword puzzles, races including horse races, card game and other game of any sort, gambling, or betting of any form whatsoever, are always taxed under this head. Lottery or prize money winnings are liable to flat rate of tax at 30% without any basic exemption limit. In such a case, the payer of prize money deducts tax at source i.e. TDS from the winnings and will pay you only the balance amount.

3. Income by way of interest received on compensation or on enhanced compensation shall be chargeable to tax under the head "Income from other sources", and such income shall be deemed to be the income of the year in which it is received, irrespective of the method of accounting followed by the assessee. However, a deduction of a sum equal to 50% of such income shall be allowed from such income. Apart from this, no other deduction shall be allowed from such an income.

Life Insurance: Any amount received under a life insurance policy, including bonus is exempt from tax under section 10(10D). However, following points should be noted in this regard.

1. Exemption is available only in respect of amount received from life insurance policy.
2. Exemption under section 10(10D) is unconditionally available in respect of sum received for a policy which is issued on or before March 31st, 2003, however, in respect of policies issued on or after April 1st, 2003, the exemption is available only if the amount of premium paid on such policy in any financial year does not exceed 20% (10% in respect of policy taken on or after April 1st, 2012) of the actual capital sum assured. It should be noted that amount received on death of the person will continue to be exempt without any condition.
3. Value of premium agreed to be returned or of any benefit by way of bonus (or otherwise), over and above the sum assured, which is received under the policy by any person, shall not be taken into

account while calculating the actual capital sum assured.

Total income from all the heads of income is called as "Gross Total Income" (GTI). To arrive at taxable income, one must deduct from GTI, the deductions allowable under Chapter VIA i.e. under section 80C to 80U. In other words, we can say that Taxable Income = Gross Total Income, less Deductions under section 80C to 80U. Following general rules should be kept in mind before claiming these deductions under section 80C to 80U:

1. No deduction under Chapter VI-A (under section 80C to 80U) shall be allowed from the following income:
    a. Long-Term Capital Gains
    b. Short-Term Capital Gains covered under section 111A
    c. Winnings from lotteries, horse race, etc., referred to in section 115BB
    d. Income covered under sections 115A, 115AB, 115AC, 115AD, 115BBA and 115D
2. The aggregate amount of deduction under section 80C to 80U cannot exceed GTI i.e., GTI excluding incomes referred to above.

[Majority of the content of the chapter on taxation has been sourced from the website of the Income Tax department of India, in accordance to this Copyright Policy published on their webpage https://www.incometaxindia.gov.in/Pages/copyright-policy.aspx, without acquiring additional and separate permissions. The copyright policy reads thus – *"Material featured on this website may be reproduced free of charge in any format or media without specific permission. However, the material has to be reproduced accurately and not be used in a derogatory manner or in a misleading context. Wherever such material is being reproduced, the source must be prominently acknowledged. The above permission to reproduce any material featured on this website shall not extend to any material featured on this website which is explicitly identified as being the copyrighted property of a third party. Authorization to reproduce such copyrighted material must be obtained from the copyright holders concerned. These terms and conditions shall be governed by and construed in accordance with the Indian Laws. Any dispute arising under these terms and conditions shall be subject to the exclusive jurisdiction of the Courts of India.*]

Progressive Execution Guide

During the glorious days of ULIPs, which were about a decade ago, some policies used to adjust entire first year premium towards fund charges. Suppose you committed to a premium of Rs. 1 Lakh per annum, in the first year, absolutely nothing would get invested. Only from the second year onwards the premiums would be invested (and certain other charges would continue throughout the term of the policy). Imagine, after paying three years premiums through the downward trend in the market and losing one-year premium as a charge, the performance of your investment was poor. If you continue the policies until maturity of the policy, you may recover your charges and make decent gain. But you panicked and discontinued the policy and received Rs. 1 Lakh against the 3 Lakhs you paid. Should we blame the investment or ourselves for our stupidity. Whether or not discontinuing the policy sensible is a subject for another time, preparing a financial plan carefully by investing time and money and when it is ready, the damage thus caused by postponing implementation of the plan citing whatever reasons is comparable to that of the ULIP situation I just described. If you cannot relate the comparison, understand that both scenarios are like pouring out your efforts through the drain. It is possible that some may find implementing entire financial plan immediately, owing to insufficient cashflows, which is understandable. But there shall be no excuse if, after knowing the repercussions of delaying key financial decisions, one does not at least start implementing the plan, beginning with risk management.

A general misconception among the financial illiterates is that financial planning is about buying financial products. Sure, it includes making investments and buying insurances, but that is not the only thing it is. If it is so, all that I have said until this point shall mean nothing. Buying financial products is the last thing one does in the elaborate process of planning for needs and goals. After all calculations have been done in line with prioritisation of needs and goals, it is time to act on the decisions, including purchase of the products. While buying or assigning products to various goals, one must be alert and make sure that maturity of the products, required rate of return and liquidity corresponding to the goals. There are also tax implications one must evaluate. While some products are taxing, some reward the buyers with tax benefits. Taxability of an investment plays a significant role in decision-making as the post-tax returns can vary between a taxable investment and an exempted one. In the section – Product Basket, we shall understand various financial products through examples and comparisons. Planning is done as precise as possible, but action plan cannot be implemented in paisa or pennies or cents. Hence, rounding off final figures to implementable level is sensible unlike how most financial planners show figures to the last rupee or dollar. So, if you come across any adviser that suggests you should invest say, Rs. 1234 or Rs. 3465 or Rs. 7698.45 etc., you can understand how practical and attentive they are in their approach. In a perfect process such as financial planning, everything counts.

Learning to plan independently

It is common today that most people, without geographical barriers, are approached by sales persons from the financial services industry, be it banking, insurance, broking, mutual funds, finance or even post office. The sales persons come by various names and designations such as relationship manager, consultant, investment adviser, life planner, agent advisor, broker etc. On an average, every individual usually meets more than one such sales professional. From the experience of having met and discussed with such professionals and sometimes combined with reading magazines, watching business news channels and browsing the internet, it is not uncommon for some people to think that financial and investment planning are easy, giving them the confidence and urge to plan their finances themselves. Others may still seek help from professionals but try to understand the terminology used by the former and ask questions to satisfy themselves that their financial decisions are not wrong. Whichever is the case, it is important for everyone, not just the professionals, to understand certain basic terminology and methods of planning, at least using the free calculators available online. In this chapter, we shall understand certain terms of personal finance and investments, go through a sample plan, learn about reviewing and what mistakes to avoid.

Meaningful Jargon

As you read the book to this point, you may have come across certain technical terms, which you might never have heard of, or if you did, you did not understand them clearly. You may also have heard some financial jargon on the television or read them in the newspapers and magazines but wondered about their significance and relevance in a contest. Referring a dictionary may not have made the meaning clear. Besides, certain words when not understood well can mislead you to appreciate them and consequently take wrong decision. Whether or not all these words have made their way into the book yet, I shall explain them in this section for better understanding. In the present world when individuals, unlike in the past are not merely celebrated but a brand in themselves, it is important that we be careful about what we read and hear, more particularly when such wisdom comes from a well-known figure. Let us understand some such jargon.

Yield

Yield is what you get from a crop. But that is agriculture. In finance, yield means different. Theoretically, straightforward, Yield is Return. But people usually like to twist it and call it earning, ratio or some other name before they call it Return. Yield is a term that is popular among the product manufacturers, distributors, and advisers. It is calculated in percentage terms and has different names and methods depending on the product. The way yield is calculated in case of stocks is different than in the case of bonds. There are variations such as dividend yield, current yield, and yield to maturity etc. While explaining yield, a professional may state that investors mistake 'total return' to 'yield' and another may say that investors mistake 'dividend yield' on stocks to 'total return' and so on. I feel it is not the investors who do not know either term that are confused, but the advisers or professionals who are burdened with exceeding terminology and in that mix-up, attribute that confusion to their clients or investors. As they explain the investors the difference between yield and total return or some other term, they may strive to clarify their own doubts. In the present context that I am going to illustrate, Return & Yield are not the same, but they are advertised as such. Once you understand the difference between the two, life will not be the same for you. I mean, your view of investments will not be the same again. Let us see the illustration.

Say, XYZ Ltd. is issuing non-convertible debentures in the market and offering 10% per annum compounded annually, for 10 years. Now, going by the tenure of the investment and the guaranteed interest rate, if Rs. 1 Lakh is invested today, at maturity one will receive 2.59 Lakhs. Now, you know 2.59 Lakhs 159% total return. Dividing 159% by 10 years, we get 15.9% or 16% per year. Is not 15.9% attractive compared to meagre 10%? But what one gets is only 10%. The 15.9% is the misleading figure that most people mistake to return. If you still have not understood, let us look at this.

Let us say KLM Bank is offering interest of 7% per annum on a 3-year fixed deposit. Do you understand it as 7% or as something else? Though the bank is offering 7%, if I ask you to treat it not as 7% but 7.50% per annum, what will be your initial reaction? Would not you say, 'do I look like a crackpot to you?' That is what exactly sales people do when they talk about yield. And if we feel good about that high yield, I have no words to describe the feeling. I do not intend to mention names in this book but, I often receive such investment opportunities on my email. One such email landed in my junk folder for a fixed deposit scheme though it did not come from the product manufacturer itself. The mailer offered a 11.91% return on a 10-year fixed deposit scheme. Doubtful and curious (not really) of such extraordinary assured return, when I clicked the advertisement, I was redirected to the company's official website and upon further digging into information, found that the return was 8% per annum that they were offering. After calculating, I was also able to arrive at 11.59% only. So, I did some more math and I was able to arrive at 11.91% exactly. Apparently, the interest, if compounded half-yearly, will give you the yield of 11.91%, even higher than 11.59% because of semi-annual compounding. You may call 11.91%, the Annualised Yield. Calling it Annualised Return may raise confusion because it means something else.

I do not say wrong about half-yearly compounding but the idea of yield in the first place (as explained in the illustration) is not very appealing to me. Is it not beautiful – the way numbers can be played with, to enthral unsuspecting investors and force them into taking unfavourable financial decisions (sometimes, the investor even shutting-up the cautious and suggesting spouse in an authoritative tone acquired from assumed superior knowledge and experience)? Now, that is the difference between 'Return' and 'Yield'. Not actually a word of caution but an earnest warning – the way sales and marketing professionals that work for commissions and incentives are becoming creative and innovative constantly, they may gradually replace the word yield with 'return' or even worse. And, there's jeopardy that you will think return is actually return but not yield. 'Return', as it is understood, fittingly refers to Compounded Annual Growth Rate. Lastly, as I explained in the reference to bank interest rate above, learn to compare return on one investment with the return on another, in percentage terms.

Absolute Return and Annualised Return

Absolute Return can also be called Total Return or Holding Period Return. It is the return on an investment calculated for the entire period it is held. For example, if you invest Rs. 50000 and after twelve months you receive back 62500, your absolute return is 25% (=(62500-50000)/50000). Suppose you hold it for 36 months and receive 72750, your holding period return for 36 months is 45.50%. In the illustration on yield, what was happening was that the holding period return or the absolute return was being averaged to a year. In this case, if 45.50% is the absolute return for three years, the annualised yield comes to 15.167%. Say, you deposited Rs. 30000 in bank for three months and receive Rs. 30750 on maturity. Your gain of Rs. 1250 calculates to a return of 2.50% per quarter. Had you made the deposit for one year i.e. four such consecutive quarters, you would have earned Rs. 3000 as interest i.e. a gain of 10% on an investment of Rs. 30000. It is a general practice to convert returns on periods that are less than one year to twelve months so as to compare with other investments conveniently and meaningfully. In this case, the 10% we have arrived at is the annualised return. But there another way to calculate it too. If you have received 2.50% in a quarter but intend to continue it for four such quarters, one may renew the entire maturity amounts starting with Rs. 30750 at the end of the first quarter, until the end of the first year, in which case, the final value at the end of year one will be Rs. 33114/- thus taking the yearly return to 10.38% instead of 10%. You may not hold the investment for four quarters but to compare the quarterly return with other investments so that you can take informed decision, the quarterly return must be annualised. This 10.38% is the Annualised Return. That is why, in the last but one paragraph of Yield, I suggested not using annualised yield and annualised return interchangeably.

Nominal Return & Effective Return

Sometimes, what may seem a straight rate of return is not the percentage that we want, to base our decision to invest. We may have to work around it a little bit to know the correct percentage. For example, if you find your bank offering interest rate of say 8% per annum compounded half yearly, that 8% is the 'Nominal Return. It is not exactly the return per annum because the interest is being compounded every six months. Say you invested Rs. 1 Lakh on which your received Rs. 4000 at the end of six months. The value at the end of six months will be Rs. 1.04 Lakh, on which 4% is calculated again for the remaining six months. At the end of twelve months, the value of the deposit will be Rs. 108160/-. The return on investment turns out to be 8.16% and not just 8.00%. This 8.16% is called the annual Effective Return. Unless an adviser or the context specifically talks about something else, the word Return usually implies Effective Return per annum. One must always be concerned about the effective return. Here, while 8% is the yearly nominal rate, 4% for six months is the half-yearly effective rate and 8.16% is the yearly effective rate. What we need is the effective return, but we need it in conjunction with the periodicity or frequency of the return too i.e. effective rate can be for a month or a quarter or half year or a year. While comparing different investments, effective rate per annum is used.

Compound Annual Growth Rate

In the simplest terms, it is interest-on-interest, which brings the word 'compound' to its name. And as the name suggests, it is usually calculated for a year for better understanding and comparing different investments but very unlikely yield and annualised return. I will not talk about the formulas to calculate CAGR here but illustrate you how it works. Some say that it is not so great because it does not capture the risk, which is altogether a different concept. If return is infused into the calculation, it is no longer a straight forward return. Once we compare investments based on return, we separately look at the risk associated with those investments and see if the return justifies the risk taken in investing in a product. Merely saying something because there is scope for something to be said whether meaningful or not will only complicate the understanding. This would be different if the discussion is with a student or professional of personal finance.

Suppose you invested Rs. 1 Lakh. After 3 years, the current value of the investment is Rs. 1.40 Lakh. CAGR of this investment calculates to 11.87%. In this example, instead of calculating the future value of the investment based on the interest or growth rate, we have done the reverse calculation i.e. finding the growth rate based on the future value. But how do we know it is correct or, what is this 11.87%? You invested Rs. 1 Lakh. By the end of the first year, it grew by 11.87% to Rs. 111870. By the end of second year, Rs. 111870 grew by 11.87% again to Rs. 125149. By the end of the third year, Rs. 125149 has grown by 11.87% to Rs. 1.40 Lakh. CAGR is used to calculate historical returns on investments and the projected, future returns. Take this example for instance. The CAGR over the last three years turned out to be 11.87%. If this return continues in the future, Rs. 1.40 Lakh will grow to Rs. 2.45 Lakhs over five years. Let us assume that the reality does not meet the expectation and the value five years hence turns out to be Rs. 2.35 Lakhs only. The CAGR for the five-year period on the investment of Rs. 1.40 Lakh works out to 10.91% and on Rs. 1 Lakh for the entire eight-year period, it works out to 11.27% per annum if the final value is Rs. 2.35 Lakhs. Check the below table that highlights the power of compounding returns in the long term and you will be impressed by its greatness.

Year	Amount	Year	Amount	Year	Amount
1	100000	11	259400	21	672700
2	110000	12	285300	22	740000
3	121000	13	313800	23	814000
4	133100	14	345200	24	895400
5	146400	15	379700	25	985000
6	161100	16	417700	26	1083500
7	177200	17	459500	27	1191800
8	194900	18	505400	28	1311000
9	214400	19	556000	29	1442100
10	235800	20	611600	30	1586300

How many years has it taken for 1 Lakh to add another lakh of rupees? Eight years, right? How much longer to add the third lakh? Four years. How long has it taken to reach the first 5-Lakh milestone? Eighteen years. And how many years did it take to make the last 5 Lakhs? Just 5 years! That is how CAGR can create wonders in the long term.

Remember, CAGR and 'long term' must go hand in hand. Independent of long term, CAGR does not seem to work at all. Is it not amazing what compounding can do? No wonder Albert Einstein called compound interest 'the eighth wonder' of the world. Compounding truly helps us only in the long term. The longer one stays invested, the higher the future value will be. But, by starting investment at say, 55 or 60, one cannot sufficiently stay invested for long term. Starting at an early age, hence, is the only solution. Therefore, if you ever hear a young person saying he is only 25 and there is a long time to plan for retirement, tell him, if he starts the investment 5 years later, he will make only 55% of what he can by starting the investment at 25. That means, if one has a target of Rs. 1 Crore retirement corpus, one will make only 55 Lakhs. Alternately we can say that if someone wanted to have an income of Rs. 30000 per month, they will have to adjust with mere 16500 per month in the old age, when they will no longer work and completely depended on this corpus.

Asset Allocation & Diversification

As the name suggests, it is allocation or apportionment of monies or finances to various asset classes. Asset Classes are many. The Common-class asset types are Equity; Debt; and Gold. The Middle-class asset types are Realty, Commodities and Foreign Exchange. The Affluent-class asset types are Art; Antiquities; Metals; Collectibles, Vintage Cars and so on. The above categorisation is only indicative and accessible and available to any person desirous and financially capable of investing in the respective asset classes. On the other hand, Diversification means spreading the investment among many companies belonging to various sectors if the asset class is equity, and if the reference is to debt, allocating the investment to bonds, debentures, fixed deposits etc. i.e. across various products or categories within the same asset class issued by different institutions.

Simple Illustration

A plan prepared by an individual himself can (by can, I mean 'it is okay to') look rugged when worked on applications like excel. So long it is well organised and easily readable, it is okay if it does not look great in print. However, a plan prepared, and report submitted by a professional can look elegant with graphics, charts and tables with added explanations and illustrations to understand the plan better. In this simple illustration, we are not looking into those aspects of polished look and design of the report but what is critical to prepare and implement a financial plan. To begin with, capture personal and family details, not because you do not know them but for calculations which depend on this throughout most of the plan.

FIRST NAME	RELATION	DATE OF BIRTH	AGE
Venkatesam	Self	25/Jul/81	38
Spouse	Wife	25/Jul/83	36
Child 1	Son	25/Jul/09	10
Child 2	Daughter	25/Jul/11	8

Do the budgeting of expenses. While doing so, also estimate old-age expenses, assuming you are retired and there are no dependants except your spouse. While taking old age (post-retirement) expenses, do not take future or inflated expenses assuming that prices will go up in the future, in the long term. Of course, they do but for now, supposing you have already retired without dependant kids, take an estimate of old age living expenses in present or today's value but give adjustments for lifestyle and age-related expenses. For example, when you are young, you may spend Rs. 5000 per month on entertainment. But when you are old, entertainment expenses may not exist, which you can remove from the budget. Alternately, you may not spend Rs. 5000 on entertainment but route it to pilgrimage. Similarly, when you are young, you may spend Rs. 3000 per month on medicines, preventive healthcare, and periodic health check-ups. But in the old age, this may double to Rs. 6000 in today's value. Also, expenses of dependant parents and children continue only until a certain age say, retirement. This must also be factored into the plan.

NATURE OF EXPENSE (MONTHLY)	TODAY	OLD AGE (P.V.)
House Rent and Maintenance	6000	6000
Groceries / Ration	4000	3000
Utilities / Bills	2000	2000
Fuel / Commutation / Maintenance	2000	1000
Health & Personal Care	500	1000
Maids / Servants	1000	500
Clothing and Accessories	2000	500
Entertainment / Vacation / Gifts	500	1000
Children & Parental Care	2000	0
Miscellaneous Expenses	0	0
TOTAL (Excl. Loans & Insurance)	**20000**	**15000**

Consider including all available incomes including interest on bank fixed deposits, dividends from mutual funds, present or future pension from immediate annuity plans, agricultural income etc., whether it is perpetual or for a limited period but be sure to note the number of years they will continue.

INCOME	P.M.	P.A.
Salary - Self	30000	360000
Salary - Spouse	10000	120000
Rent	5000	60000
TOTAL	**45000**	**540000**

Get all your loan statements containing interest and principal break-up, outstanding principal on the date of working the calculation, probable charges in case of pre-closure etc. This should include temporary liabilities such as credit card outstanding (whether defaulted or not) and overall limit but not the outstanding if the card is used for regular monthly spending that is immediately repaid.

TYPE	LOAN	DATE	TERM	RATE	EMI	O/S
Housing Loan	1000000	1/Apr/09	20	10.00%	9650	856000

If you are in public or private service i.e. employment of some organisation working for fixed or variable salary or both, go through your service agreements, offer or appointment letters, pay-scale structures, and list all the benefits provided by your employer. Details may look like those in the below table. Try to write down as much information as you can.

BENEFIT	SELF	SPOUSE
Current Basic Salary	10000	5000
Current balance in EPF/EPS	100000	50000
Current contribution to EPF/EPS	2400	1200
Completed years of service till date	8	4

Future years of service	2	1
Years to retirement after leaving	20	19
Basic at the time of leaving service	11000	5000
Life Insurance from employer	500000	250000
Health Insurance from employer	200000	200000
Accidental Insurance cover	500000	250000

Identify your investment risk profile – risk tolerance or risk appetite and draw your asset allocation for investments towards various needs and goals. Let us say that based on the expected return from individual asset classes, the required portfolio return, which may or may not help you achieve your needs but matches with your risk profile, calculates to 9.60 %. This means, that you must allocate all investments among the three asset classes shown in chart in the previous page in the recommended percentages. However, this may not apply to existing investments if you cannot redeem them and reinvest for reasons whatever

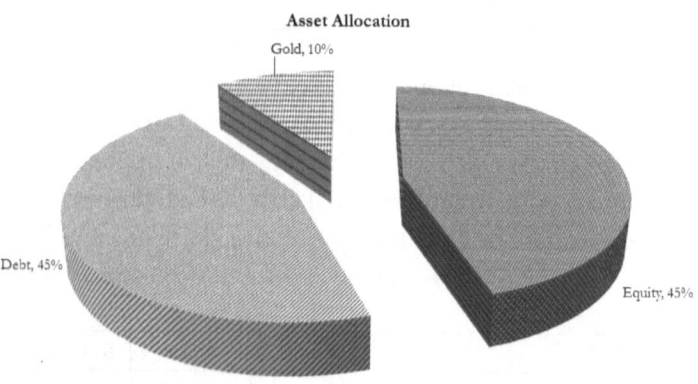

Life insurance is the foremost requirement in any financial plan. The need for life insurance is above all other financial

needs and goals. In the absence of life insurance, the dependents will have to survive for a long time without adequate income. Hence, identifying the Human Life Value is the first thing to determine life insurance requirement.

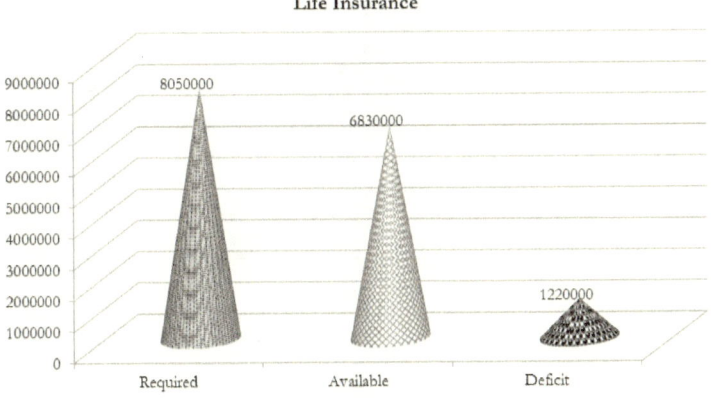

Life Insurance

ADD	
Lifetime living / household expenses of Family	5330000
Discounted cost of all children future needs	1863000
Outstanding loans and liabilities	856000
Total Life Insurance requirement	**8050000**

LESS	
Present value of Spouse's income till retirement	2640000
Existing Sum Assured across life plans (self)	500000
Present value of all investments and insurance plans	752000
Present value of all perpetual incomes like Rent etc.	2940000
Total of existing provisions including liquid assets	**6830000**

Additional Life Insurance cover to be bought	**1220000**

Find out how long will the existing provisions will support the family's expenses, if you do not buy additional life insurance cover by the amount that you are underinsured. In the below table you can see that the current provisions of Rs. 68.30 Lakhs will provide until the age of 65 only while the spouse has a life expectancy of 85 years i.e. for the next 20 years, the spouse will have to live the life of a destitute under the grace and charity of someone else or if you have any property and jewellery, sell them for her survival.

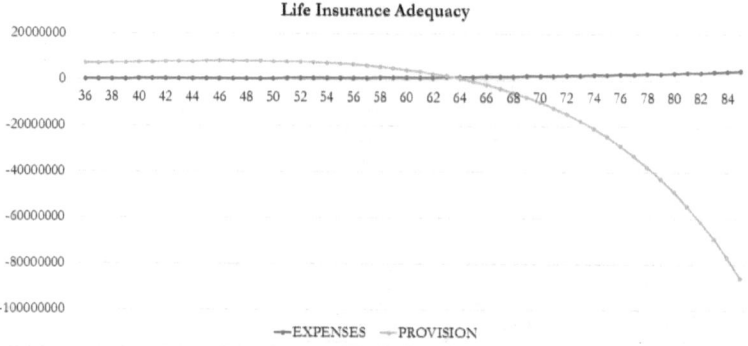

Similarly, calculate Disability Insurance, Health Insurance and Critical Illness Insurances requirements and compare premiums and features of policies across life insurance companies, for the quantum of need.

Risk Management Summary	Amount
Life Insurance cover required to cover living expenses before retirement	3700000
Life Insurance cover required to cover living expenses after retirement	1630000
Disability Insurance required to cover living / household expenses	7400000

Health Insurance required to cover hospitalization expenses	300000
Critical Illness Insurance required to cover terminal illness expenses	1500000
Old Age Medical Emergency fund required by Retirement age	4100000

It is a general view of the average person that retirement is (not mostly) but only about pension or getting regular income after retirement. However, in real, there is more to retirement than just sitting in an easy chair in the lawn and enjoying life while you get your monthly pension deposited into your bank. This is how you make provisions to your retirement corpus.

CURRENT PROVISIONS	**SELF**	**SPOUSE**
Gratuity while leaving service	63,000	14,000
Gratuity invested till retirement	3,77,000	76,500
EPF balance while leaving service	1,80,000	68,000
EPF invested till retirement	10,80,000	2,93,000
EFP held for entire service	30,00,000	15,00,000
Retirement corpus required	1,76,00,000	
Existing provisions made from all sources	1,69,00,000	
Deficit in Retirement corpus	700,000	
To fill the deficit, invest additionally (p.a.)	9800	
To fill the deficit, invest additionally (p.m.)	800	

Besides pension, an individual may have many other financial goals and needs that he wants / needs to plan for, such as higher education or wedding. For the estimated present value/cost, calculate the future value, allocate various existing investment to the goals, and check if any additional investment is required to be made – a one time or recurring.

GOAL	YEARS	P.V.	F.V.	PLANNED	DEFICIT	INVEST
Child 1 Education	11	500000	1400000	407000	993000	4300
Child 2 Education	13	300000	1000000	511000	489000	1600
Child 1 Wedding	22	500000	2700000	1820000	880000	1000
Child 2 Wedding	20	800000	3700000	1790000	1910000	2800

Besides children's needs, you may have other financial goals. Though you calculate the need initially, based on priority, at the time of implementation, you may make modifications to the goals as you find comfortable. Compare the below two goals – apartment and car with children goals. Assuming your cashflow has limited surplus that cannot accommodate all goals, even if you scrap the wedding goals to accommodate car or house, the amount you will save will be just 2800 + 1000 = 3800 while the car goal requires investment of Rs. 5200. Try to work around the figures and see if you can postpone the car goal for say another 2 years. Since the wedding goals are exceedingly long time away, you may consider postponing investments for wedding until the car goal is achieved. By then, your income will have increased by a good percentage to allocate higher amounts to wedding goals, as the period will be down by 5 or 7 years as you plan it.

GOAL	YEARS	P.V.	F.V.	PLANNED	DEFICIT	INVEST
Apartment	10	500000	1100000	216000	884000	4500
Car	5	300000	400000	0	400000	5200

As explained in the above paragraph, to know if various cash inflows cater to the financial needs and goals adequately, and whether any goals will have to be trimmed, you need to prepare a cashflow statement. Now that you have all the cash inflows and outflows viz. various recurring incomes, household expenses, loan instalments, current and proposed insurance premiums, goal outflows forming part of net income (e.g. EPF is not to be counted or else the calculations will become comprehensive and more difficult for a novice to manage), and needs such as annuity and old age medicals. It helps preparing the cashflow table in Microsoft Excel file with columns such as age, own income, spouse's income, other income (each separately), household expenses, retirement, children goals, other goals, insurances and so on. Once you look at the cashflow report and know whether you have net surplus or deficit, you make necessary modifications or be content with the current allocation. If you have significant surplus, it is up to you to rework the plan so as to choose less riskier investments for lower return, increase regular investment for a goal to achieve it faster or to accumulate more wealth, add another goal that you initially pushed aside etc.

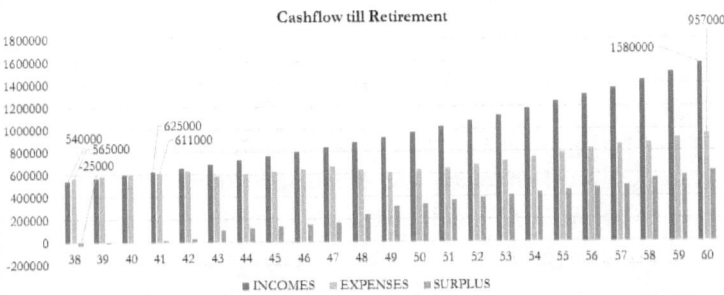

To make the entire plan simple to look at, finally, create an Action Plan that contains summary of all financial needs and goals one by one. Preparing one- or two-page summary by goal and writing down all the steps to be taken pertaining to that gives a quick view of the entire plan. Points you may jot down include monthly investment to be made or premium payable, financial products across which the new investment should be diversified, action against existing products such as withdrawal or surrender etc. Once you have the action plan, you do not need to revisit the entire comprehensive plan for implementation but always refer the summary. The plan may be reviewed and revised periodically after some lapse from the time you first prepared the plan. Usually, that is most what an individual is concerned about. However, if the plan is prepared by a professional for a client, it may contain additional pages covering detailed risk-profiling questionnaire, analysis of risk profile and reasoning for selecting an asset allocation strategy, standard and statutory mentions such as a letter establishing the relationship between the planner and client, a non-disclosure agreement, etc.

Keeping in shape on the track

You have read so much so far, which I believe I have expressed plainly. If you are a student or an aspiring professional, you now know the characteristics of a true financial planner and if you are an individual looking to organise your finances, you understand how to go about the process while avoiding mistakes, a few of which are also mentioned in the next section. Let us suppose that you have prepared a plan and implemented the action plan as illustrated above. Is that all there is to it? No, financial planning does not end with mere implementation of the initial conclusions. It is a continuous process. Changes are constant in the material world, be it the nature, plant life or animal kingdom. Human life is no different and so are personal finances. Some changes happen for good and some may have neutral effect on the finances. But some changes can have harsh effects on financial lives. It is therefore important that periodically, such changes be accommodated in the plan to keep it goal-oriented, achievable and on the right track. But what are these changes and what does review involve? Review is of two types viz. Plan Review and Portfolio Review.

Periodic Review

Who know that they will have another child a few years after the first born? People think that they can plan it, but the truth is, for most traditional families in India, knowing and thinking about planning for a child is a beautiful lie. For them, it just happens. You were so precise that while you worked on the plan you made provisions for a job change after ten years, expecting a 30% hike from the prospective employer. But when the time comes, your employer retains you by giving 50% hike and other perks, which permanently influences your cashflows for the rest of your life by a significant difference. Or, you moved to another organisation expecting a 30% hike as per your plan but out of the blue, you receive 75% hike on your last pay. You planned for your child's higher education in engineering or robotics or artificial intelligence. You thought the child will have to study in a world-class university and made provisions that will give you say, Rs. 1 Crore twenty years hence. But at the age of fifteen, you son wants to become an artist or a musician or even better, a writer. How much does that cost – a paint brush or pencil, a pen or at most a musical instrument? What will you do with the 1 Crore? Five years before the goal, when you have Rs. 75 Lakhs already accumulated, your child pours water on the fire. What will you do with that money? You do not just give it away to the child as you feel that he will not make a living out of such a profession he or she chooses. You need proper planning. Changes like these can happen in anybody's life and these are not small. They have a great and permanent impact on the future of the entire financial plan and the personal finances of the family. Either the change will leave us with excess money, or it will load additional expenses, further straining the tight cashflows. This is where financial plan review comes into picture. Whenever a major life event occurs that can impact entire financial future of the family, the entire plan must be reviewed and if need be, restructured to suit the changes. This need not be done at regular intervals i.e. once every year or once every three years or so. It can be done whenever such a change pops up. If there are no such excitements in life that need special attention, the originally designed plan must be left to continue. Let us take another scenario. Few years before retirement, you should again do the budgeting and see how your prediction has fared. I mean to say that you should check how expenses have inflated and how your life style has changed over the years. And, since you are remarkably close to retirement, you have a better idea of what your post-retirement expenses will be. Let me explain. Say, when you first planned at 30 your retirement, you projected that your then expenses of 30000 per month would inflate to 1.60 Lakhs. However, at 55 when you checked your expenses, you are spending 2 Lakhs a month. The reason obviously is inflation but the higher than expected rise in expenses can be due to the improved lifestyle also. In the beginning, you thought you would spend the same amount (adjusted for inflation) at 60 that you spent at 30. However, early progress in your career changed your lifestyle too. And now, accustomed to your improved lifestyle, you may find it difficult to compromise on your expenses in old age. So, you need to rework the budget you proposed for post-retirement life and see how far the proposed retirement corpus will support you in meeting the old age expenses. If there is any chance, you may try to recoup the difference during the last few years of earning phase.

That is one side of the review. Let us assume there are no such major influential changes in life. Yet, periodic review must be done. But that review is not that of the financial plan but for the portfolio of investments and other financial products purchased. Once investments have been made as per the decided asset allocation, the individual products must be periodically reviewed for fundamental changes. The fund manager may change. One company in which we invested may merge with another and the new management may replace the existing team that is completely new and lacks history to deduce anything. Government may cut down interest rate on certain product such as the provident fund not just for a fiscal year that is usually done but permanently and that too, retrospectively, or it may even review certain sections of the Income Tax Act and withdraw tax benefits on certain tax-saving investments. Once such incident happened in 2018, which was reintroduction of long-term capital gains tax on equity, after many years. If not that, at least a fund manager who has been know to play safe by investing in predominantly large cap companies and holding for long term in a multi-cap scheme may suddenly change gear and increase allocation to mid and small cap companies and not just that, he may start taking short term calls in order to fight competition from the peers and deliver superior returns to the investors. Thought the scheme is a multi-cap fund that naturally allows a fund manager to invest anywhere within certain limits, our decisions influenced by experience must be reviewed occasionally to ensure if the products are suitable for our goals or not. While doing so, one must also consider rebalancing the portfolio as per the initially decided asset allocation strategy. For example, you settled that you should always maintain 70% of the portfolio in equity, be it shares or mutual funds or unit-linked plans. After a while, you find that the equity portion has far exceeded this limit due to extraordinary market performance and stands at 85%, because of which, the allocation to other asset classes, perhaps debt and gold have significantly gone down steeply. You reduce the allocation to equity by 15% and adjust it between debt and gold. Suppose, the market has not fared well, and your equity allocation has gone down by 10%. You dilute some portion of debt and gold and add it to equity, which means buying low during a bear market. However, such rebalancing must be done as per the initially decided risk profile and its related asset allocation strategy. Doing it just because it seems lucrative in the prevailing market scenario or someone did or recommended it may hurt later, financially, and irreversibly.

Avoiding Mistakes

All of us make mistakes at some point of time in our lives. Some mistakes do not affect us much but there are some that will haunt us for the rest of our lives either directly or indirectly. Here, I am not referring to the emotional and sentimental kind of mistakes. I am referring more to the irreversible financial decisions we take in our lives that we repent in the later years. Though I mentioned about planning in the previous chapters, there is more to be careful about, when it comes to retirement planning. Just type in the words 'retirement planning' and hit the search button on Google. I did the same and was astounded by the number of results I got – a mere 3.33 Billion. And, the first three pages have nothing but links mostly to various life insurance companies and some online calculators.

Mistake 1

Okay. Now that I have raised the topic, first let me update you on the calculator's part. Very comfortably, if your search for those, you'll find lot many online tools or calculators that ask you to enter certain figures or information in some fields provided on the website or just move some sliders to the left and right, upon doing which, you'll be told how much retirement corpus you need and blah, blah, blah. In addition to these, many organizations in the business of financial advisory services tend to offer 'free' retirement or financial planning services. You may be thinking, 'what's bad or wrong if someone's offering a good thing for free?' What can I say? There is no such thing as free lunch! Just ask yourself. What do they, those who are offering professional advice and services free, get if they give you something free? There should be something in it for them! Yes, there is. Most of the free advices and services come with implied conditions. Once you fill the form or give your details, a free plan or advice or report is created and discussed with you patiently. Then, when you trust the approach and advice of the relationship manager or the organization, the advices start pouring in. It begins with, 'Sir, now that you have the plan, why not to implement it without much delay? At least, let us start with something. This product is good for you or suits your requirement. You should go with this. This is a beautiful product and the last date is fast approaching for this and you won't be able to invest in this later'. Now, nothing is bad with that as long as the adviser, the relationship manager, or the organization has no vested interest in the products they are recommending. When you are reluctant to buy the products, you will get more options. You will start receiving emails and soon, your mailbox will be flooded with illustrations of products recommended for you. Eventually, you will buy those irrespective of the amount or you will change your mobile and email. But for them, the companies, and advisors, it is worth a shot. Because the commission or brokerage is so impressive, that they do not feel the pinch when they offer you certain advice for 'free'. But that is only on one side of the coin. Now, let us look at the other side. Let us say, the online free retirement calculator or the free financial plan, after you put in some details, gives you a figure. Say, you are 40 years old and want to retire at 60. Your monthly retirement expenses are 50000 in today's value. Supposing that your life expectancy is 85, the tool or the report shows that you must accumulate retirement corpus of 6.50 Crores approximately and for that, you should invest 1 Lakh a month. You may be earning well but saving 1 Lakh a month i.e. 12 Lakhs per annum may not be so easy. Come on! How am I going to do that? You get the reply, 'how should I know? This is what you need to invest. If you cannot or if you do not, then you will suffer', not literally of course. The free tool or report does not tell you most of the time, what you need to do or what could be done if you want to have a worry-free retired life. They do not thoroughly evaluate your current contributions to the fund. They do not suggest alternatives. A fee-based advisor on the other hand gives multiple options. Say, you cannot invest 1 Lakh. He will check with you and explain how it will look like, if you cut down your expenses. Let us suppose you do not want to compromise with your expenses in old age. Then you will be asked, by giving the future picture, if you will postpone your retirement by say, x number of years. You say you do not want to prolong your retirement. Then, another option is given to you. For a very long-term goal like this, if you allocate more monies to high-risk products, you will be able to achieve the required retirement corpus by investing lesser amount. But you say 'no' to that too. You do not want to risk the monies meant for your old age expenses. You get another option, and so on so forth. A fee-only advisor can help you until the end and show you how the goal can be achieved without difficulty. So, *the first mistake you should not be doing is, falling for 'free'*. There is no such thing as 'free lunch'.

Mistake 2

It is acceptable if you have not started investing in the right places towards your financial needs, only if you are not aware of the urgency or the exact requirement or the strategies. But there is no other sin when it comes to personal finances, that is worse than investing late (with an exception). You may have read about this concept of investing early but, I shall still take you through that. Let us take an example here. Mr A, 30 years old, starts investing for his retirement a sum of 10000 per month. His colleague Mr B, 40 years old realising the need late, started investing 15000 per month to compensate the time loss. Both, Mr A and Mr B plan to retire at the age of 60. When they retired, Mr A has 1.97 Crore and Mr B, who invested 50% more (to compensate the time loss) than what Mr A did, has 1.03 Crore in hand i.e. just 52% of fund Mr A has. Surprisingly, even if Mr B invested 20000 i.e. double of what Mr A invested, his fund will be only 1.37 Crore or 70% of the fund value of Mr A. So, **the second mistake you should not be doing is, to start investing late towards retirement.** Now that you know the impact of investing late, if you are already old enough it is better to start immediately. And, if you are young, there is no better time to start investing for retirement than now. In either case, the mantra is 'start early'.

Mistake 3

In every meeting, whether I am addressing a group or interviewing an individual client, I ask the listener what he thinks the rate of inflation in the long term is. And, I usually get replies like 5%, 6%, 10%, 12% etc. When I ask them how they come up with that figure, they say that they just assumed or read it in the news etc. Some knowledgeable individuals say that the practical inflation is far more than what RBI declares every now-and-then. True. What RBI declares regularly is the growth in the wholesale price index and the consumer price index – the two leading indicators for tracking inflation in India. Remarkable modifications have been made by the RBI in these inflation indices in the past decade but still, it feels that the inflation we experience is more than what the central bank announces. However, if going by this leading economic indicator, inflation is calculated based on the index points for lengthy periods of

25 or 30 years, the average comes to 7%. One can, to be on the safer side, hike it to 8% so that if the assumption goes wrong in such longer periods. When the needs are of long term in nature (15, 20, 25 years), it does not make sense to the weekly or yearly inflation rates you see on the television. Hence, this long-term theory. But, why is it so important to be precise when assuming inflation rate or for that matter returns on investments or any other such percentage? What happens if there is slight deviation by say a percentage point or so? Let us find out. Let us take retirement as example. Suppose an individual aged 35 wants to retire at 58. His expenses if retired, are 40000/- per month (4.80 Lakhs p.a.). By his retirement age, these expenses will have inflated to 2.54 Lakhs p.m. or 30 Lakhs p.a. Let us say, the risk-free rate of return in the long term will be 8% p.a. If we fall in 30% tax slab (as per today's laws), the net return will be 5.5% p.a. Inflation adjusted (Real Rate) return is -2.30% p.a. To be able to meet that kind of inflating expense, he will need to create retirement corpus of 10.75 Crores in 25 years. Now, the tricky part! What if we assume that inflation rate in the long term will be only 6% instead of 8%? Nothing much, but the retirement corpus requirement will be just 5.30 Crores as opposed to 10.75 Crores we arrived at above. This shows us that in the long term, a difference in 2% inflation will change the figures by 100%. Let us apply the same principle to investments. We buy a life insurance policy expecting 8.5% returns p.a. But, at maturity, the average turns out to be 6% p.a. This means that, when we are expecting say, 1 Lakh, we will receive just 47000/- The question is, can we afford to take this kind of chances?!!! Where will you suddenly bring that kind of money from? How will you double the money in just less than one year, for which you took 25 years to accumulate? So, ***the third and***

most devastating mistake you should never be making is making inappropriate assumptions. At least when you assume something, do so by correctly interpreting the facts. Or, the best thing is to seek professional assistance. Surely, paying a few thousands to a professional for the genuine advice is nothing compared to the probable losses you may incur by doing things wrongly.

Mistake 4

A professional becomes so, just like you did, with years of education, experience, study, and research. You may be software a professional, a doctor, or an engineer with a grasp of financial terminology and methods. But you are not a financial professional. Just like how experts from other professions cannot advise you on your line of work, so cannot you when it comes to financial planning. I am not saying that you cannot manage your monies on your own. All I am saying is that you should leave the job of advising on personal finances to the practicing professionals and not take matters into your own hands. Sharing wrong things, which you assume to be right, can leave long lasting impression on others that will only harm them. You may have experience in equity investment. You made decent gains and at times, you incurred losses. You have some tips and know some tricks when it comes to investing. Use them on your own monies and investments. Do not offer free advice to your colleagues, family, relatives, and friends even if they regard you as the guru of personal finance. And, if someone asks you, humbly advise them to seek professional help and if you know any, refer them. Never take matters into your own hands if you cannot take the moral responsibility of the results and consequences others will face. So, ***the*** *fourth mistake you must not make is undervaluing a professional's experience and subject matter expertise, unless proven otherwise.*

Mistake 5

It is last quarter of the fiscal year and everyone in your office is submitting tax declaration along with the proofs. You too must make some investment to cut down your tax liability. Unfortunately, you do not know which financial product to buy or invest. Luckily, you saw a colleague filling up some forms and enquired with him. He told you he is investing in mutual fund or some life insurance policy. The relationship manager who came to your colleague for collecting the forms was sitting right there. You asked him if it is good and the advisor says it is the best. You jump in joy, relieved that now you too can submit the tax declaration before deadline. You also fill up the forms and write a cheque and hand over the documents to the relationship manager, who too was jumping in joy in his heart for he got two birds in one shot. I bet most of the readers must have found themselves in this kind of situation at some point of time in the past – near or far. If you have not liked the story above, then that is what you should not be doing. I should share an example here with you. Few years back I had a client, a young man. I educated him about investments and various strategies, what he should do and what not. For two years, I taught him. And, one day when I met him, he was almost crying. He said, in hurry, he bought a ULIP and the company deducted the entire first year premium of 1 Lakh towards fund management charges. Not ignoring the fact that fate plays the ultimate role in our lives, we must be utmost careful when taking financial decisions that will financially and psychologically influence us in the days to come. What I mean to say is, do not imitate your friends or colleagues when making investments or buying financial products. Your friend who is investing in equity oriented, midcap mutual fund scheme may have years of experience and understands the standard deviation (or simply, portfolio risk) well and since he understands it well, if the investment performs poorly, it will not pinch him in the heart because he already anticipated that when he made the investment. He knows the probability and has the appetite for risk. So, when you ask him, with the confidence he got from experience and tolerance for risk, he suggested you go ahead and invest in the same product as he did. Sometime later, when you checked the performance, you saw that the return is -5% or 10%. You are worried and regret taking your friend's advice and not leaving it there, you curse him inside and strain your relationship with him besides losing on your investment. Now you know what you should not be doing, don't you? Then, there is this other case. Again, I should share my experience here. An uncle of mine, when we met after a long time, in our discussion, mentioned that he invested in xyz policy. He said that the agent advised him to invest for three years, after which he can discontinue the investment. Three years later, the uncle found the investment in its worst shape, some 80% less to the aggregate investment. The first thing he did was, redeem the investment at 80% loss to the principal. It is not just my uncle. In my interactions with many individual clients, I found they did the same thing. When you invest, you ask the agent questions relating to the risk, expected returns, investment strategy etc. But, when the investment does not perform, you do not call to that agent or advisor and if the agent cannot be reached, call the company, and ask what to do. At least if you charge them with giving wrong advice, they would explain you and direct you on the actions you need to take. But people just do not do it. They just sell it for a loss and keeping the wrong on their side, they accuse the agents, the company, and the product. Shortly after giving presentation on financial planning in a private firm recently, I received a call from one of the attendees. The lady called me and said that she had some investments of ABC Company. She said that a relationship manager came to her along with the branch manager of the bank where the lady has her salary account. The branch manager advised her to invest in something and she, trusting him for the office he held, made the investment. She was not aware that there's risk cover in the investment and that out of the 1.50 Lakh she invested in three years, 50000 was charged as risk premium besides other charges. I hope you now got the message from the above cases. So, **the fifth mistake you should avoid making is, depending on unprofessional advice, and taking uninformed decisions**. Know and believe that one solution does not suit all.

Mistake 6

Over the years, I came across individuals who availed services of financial planners freely or for a fee. In cases where the service or advice was received free, I can understand. But, where people bought the services for a good fee, the one thing that they ignored was the implementation. I already mentioned before in this book that no plan is worth a dime unless it is put into action. A financial plan or in the present context, a retirement plan must be implemented when it has been made. Every single day you delay, the purpose of the exercise is lost. I am not implying that if you do not have money, you should borrow to invest. Having the plan does not mean you have money to invest too. But it is best to start implementation of the plan any way you can. Say, if you need to invest 15000 a month, and you have surplus monies of just 3000, start with that. As and when your short-term commitments have been fulfilled and when you can see additional monies in your hand again, you should diversify as required by the plan. Also, during my encounters with prospective clients, I hear a lot like - 'I invested in this product to save tax or reduce my tax liability'. Fine, but what is your objective in buying this? I told you, it must save tax. Now, if the reader has been in this situation, this is my question to you. If tomorrow (I mean, in the future), your investment gives you negative returns meaning you investment value goes down sharply by say, 50%, will you be happy? I say you should be happy. You know why? Because, you wanted to save tax and mind you, the moment you made the investment, you saved on tax. So, if that is your objective, you should be happy whether you gain or lose on your investment, right? But, will you be genuinely happy? Of course, not! And why, because it is your hard-earned money and you have lot of hopes on it, doing well. It pinches you in the heart when the investment does not do well. That pinch and pain in the heart is because, saving on tax is not your only objective let alone the main one. So, this is how it should have been if you did not want to feel the pain. You identified the need, quantified it, applied the inflation rate, figured out how much you will need in the future, and then calculated the monies required to be invested at a desired rate of return and then made the investment after careful study. And, before you invested, you ensured that the product you chose also gave the tax benefits you required. Had you done this, the decline in the value of your investment in the short term would not have bothered you. When you did not do it this way, it would seem as if you were not concerned whether you gained or lost. So, ***the sixth mistake you should not be doing is to invest or buy financial products with the primary objective of saving tax.***

Mistake 7

What if the fund manager you always held in the highest regard leaves the company for a better opportunity where you made an investment or has been promoted and entrusted with a higher responsibility by his employer that does not involve fund management? And, you are not even aware that this person has been replaced by some other fund manager from within the organization or recruited from elsewhere? Or, the fund manager suddenly shifts the fund strategy, though within the purview of the defined and originally declared method. Let us say, in a flexi-cap fund, he has been allocating monies to large-cap and you invested in the fund. Over a period, the fund manager gradually increases allocation to midcap and brings down the holding in large cap to comparatively low levels. And, you are not comfortable with that kind of risk. What will happen to your investment can be expected but the question is, are you okay with that? Forgetting for the moment the fact that the above situations may have a terrible impact on your investments, how would you cope if you do not even track the changes or follow-up with the news that pertain to your investment? Again, I am not implying that you should do all this demanding work yourself. But you need to talk to someone, read about the changes that result in transformation of the industry in the long term etc. If you do not, you and your investment will be left out. Believe me, even the product manufacturers and fund houses do not concentrate on their own products and investments that are lagging in performance, let alone the distributors, brokers and agents. They only try to sell and make money from the performing ones (where they can show you attractive figures) and the 'new' (where they do not need to show any attractive figures). No one respects and care about the weak and non-performers. We already discussed what 'new' means. So, **the seventh mistake you must not make is to break away from the happenings in the financial services industry.** And, when you do as you are advised, you should not coo over petty returns you make in the short term, nor should you cry over the unrealized losses.

Mistake 8

This is not exactly a mistake but about something where your actions must be logical and make sense. It is something to bring you out of confusion and give you clarity. Often, I heard from people that they are confused about the investment tenure. They say that their advisor or relationship manager told them that if for example they start a systematic investment plan, they should apply for three or five years only. And at the end of the period, they should review and start a new investment. Personally (and professionally), I do not see the logic behind doing this. I do not mean the reviewing part but the period of investment. If anyone has objection about the period of investment, it should be in case of products where there is no liquidity or where the person made a commitment to invest regularly for a certain period. Suppose you are buying a life insurance plan. As insurance plans usually have a term to maturity that you are free to choose but with the risk of devastating loss in case of surrender, you must be careful while selecting the term. You must know whether you will be able to pay the premiums for five years, ten years, or fifteen years etc. In such a case, if you need money in the middle and want to surrender the policy, the surrender proceeds you get will make you weep. But that is not the case with products where you have liquidity. Let us say you started a systematic investment plan in an equity-oriented mutual fund scheme. The fund is so liquid, that you can, any time during the period of investment, decide to stop the SIP or altogether exit the investment, having to pay an exit load only when you withdraw within twelve months from the date of investing. When you have such an option, how does it matter whether you apply for three years, five years, or fifty years? You apply for lifetime (99 years). And, suppose three years later you find it unfavourable or unattractive, submit a request to stop further investment into the scheme. It is as simple as that. As to the review, you can do it any time whether you are investing in the fund or not. Nobody stops you from researching and reviewing a particular investment. But certain products like insurance plans and small savings schemes make it compulsory to invest for certain minimum period and do not have an early exit option. So, ***the eight mistake you should not be doing is to buy financial products without relating the term of the product and liquidity to the goal.***

Wrap-up

That concludes most financial planning principles and strategies. I may have skipped a few and might have missed a few but anything that is fundamental and critical to a secured financial future has not been missed in the six chapters of this book. I have also avoided the monotonous style to not bore the reader, be it a student or an individual seeking personal financial wisdom and hope you have enjoyed reading the book. Nevertheless, certain subjects such as taxation and references to laws cannot be discussed without the original texts, which may appear vague or difficult to follow in some areas. But that should not dissuade discourage the reader for, the rules of tax law and other principles alongside other subjects talked-about in this book are of utmost importance for individuals, particularly in whose interest it has been written and published.

Though we are past the discussions in this book already, I shall again repeat one aspect about this subject. Financial planning can be done as elaborately as one can imagine. But it may not always be so necessary to do tiresome calculations. For example, tax planning is an integral part of the financial planning process but it may not be necessary to first do petty calculations such as that of the house rent allowance in order to arrive at net salary income, which will be appreciated at a certain percentage throughout the earning phase, to workout the cashflows. A carefully drafted plan may not need review or reworking every year unless there is a major event or situation that will impact the entire financial future. However, it must not be mistaken that one's tax liability need not be calculated thoroughly every year, which is an exercise different from long-term financial planning. One can keep it as simple or make it as complex as one wishes but must be wary that consolidation of figures into simpler ones does not exert undue effect on the plan.

The entire book has been written to convince and make the reader understand the importance of the below aspects of personal financial planning in the below given order and implement the action plan for a secured financial future.

1. Budgeting of all expenses and incomes in detail to make preliminary cashflow projections
2. Make provisions for critical risks such as death, disability, and terminal illness
3. Plan to use any surplus to clear overdue liabilities or create surplus by tailoring budget
4. Insure secondary risks such as health insurance, household items etc.
5. Identify investment risk tolerance and appetite, and decide an asset allocation method
6. List the financial needs and goals other than insurance, prioritize and quantify them
7. Make logical estimates of inflation and return rates that will affect various needs and goals
8. Analyse and evaluate financial needs and goals and develop the plan

9. Identify suitable financial products that are in sync with goal time horizon and other needs
10. Implement the action plan and review periodically or in cases of major life and financial events

Seek the help of a professional in developing the plan. Attend the meeting with the financial planner, together with the spouse. Do not shun from paying a fee to the planner. Suppose you spend Rs. 1000 per month on entertainment or even say employing a house cleaner. The expenditure increases by 200 per month every year. In 25 years, you will have spent Rs. 10.20 Lakhs. Alternately, say you pay Rs. 10000 as initial fee to the financial planner and from second year onward, pay review fee of Rs. 3000, increasing it by 500 every year. You will have paid a total of Rs. 02.20 Lakhs to the planner in 25 years. If you have understood how much a financial planner can contribute to your financial wellbeing, you will know how much fee is reasonable. Financial planners charge a flexible fee that is different from person to person. In the US, planners advise on hourly basis also. The average hourly fee may be USD 200 that converts to Rs. 14000 per hour. If a plan takes 10 hours to complete, the fee can be Rs. 1.40 Lakh, which can equal the expenses of a lower middle-class family. Though the hourly fee system is not prevalent in India, a handful of advisers may charge anywhere between Rs. 500 to Rs. 1000 per hour. So, next time if you hear anyone cribbing about USD-INR foreign exchange rates and want everything at par with USD, tell them to think it over. We may not be able to match the currencies, but we can inflate the expenses to match the US prices. Of course, that is on a lighter note and for those who are not willing to learn and accept what economists have to say.

Financial planning is in everything for, it is more about common sense that has more inclination towards money matters besides other situations. If there is a new iPhone launch and you cannot afford it right away, plan for the next model after two years and start a recurring deposit in a bank or a systematic investment plan of Rs. 4000 or $ 70 per month for two years in a mutual fund scheme. If you must create a contingency fund of Rs. 3 Lakhs, savings account gives 4% return, which is exempt from tax up to Rs. 10000 per annum i.e. Rs. 2000 is taxable at say 20% plus 4% cess bringing down the net return to 3.467%. Alternately, by sacrificing liquidity for 24 hours (withdrawal notice 24 hours in advance) liquid mutual fund can give 7.50% return and after say 20% short-term capital gains tax and 4% cess, the net return will be 5.94% i.e. a yearly post-tax return of Rs. 17820 as opposed to Rs. 10400 on savings bank. The difference of Rs. 7400 extra return per year if reinvested in equity at 12% for 25 years will give 11 Lakhs in the future. If the future probability does not impress you and you are more concerned with the present, not respecting the extra gain of Rs. 7400 can equal buying 85 Litres of petrol from the station once every year and dumping it in the sewer. The trend has not yet spread to India but in certain geographies, a financial planner may even advise whether one should divorce one's spouse or not, what to study at the university, what business to start and so on, depending on the experience of the professional. That is Financial Planning!

That is all about it. I hope you have enjoyed reading it and understood the crux of the subject. It is now time to act for a better future for yourself and your many later generations to come. Good luck!

www.ingramcontent.com/pod-product-compliance
Lightning Source LLC
Chambersburg PA
CBHW020735180526
45163CB00001B/251